Home Movies
and Other Necessary Fictions

VISIBLE EVIDENCE

Edited by Michael Renov, Faye Ginsburg, and Jane Gaines

Public confidence in the "real" is everywhere in decline. This series offers a forum for the in-depth consideration of the representation of the real, with books that engage issues that bear upon questions of cultural and historical representation, and that forward the work of challenging prevailing notions of the "documentary tradition" and of nonfiction culture more generally.

Volume 4 :: Michelle Citron
           Home Movies and Other Necessary Fictions
Volume 3 :: Andrea Liss
           Trespassing through Shadows:
           Memory, Photography, and the Holocaust
Volume 2 :: Toby Miller
           Technologies of Truth:
           Cultural Citizenship and the Popular Media
Volume 1 :: Chris Holmlund and Cynthia Fuchs, editors
           Between the Sheets, In the Streets:
           Queer, Lesbian, Gay Documentary

VISIBLE EVIDENCE, VOLUME 4

Home Movies and Other Necessary Fictions

Michelle Citron

University of Minnesota Press

Minneapolis

London

Published with assistance from the Margaret S. Harding Memorial Endowment honoring the first director of the University of Minnesota Press.

Speaking the Unspeakable: How We Talk When Words Fail was first delivered as a performance piece for the *Van Zelst Communication Report,* Northwestern University, November 10, 1992. *The Simple Act of Seeing* was first delivered as a performance piece for the Chicago Institute for Psychoanalysis, Chicago Cultural Center, May 1993.

Daughter Rite and *What You Take For Granted* . . . are available from Women Make Movies, Inc., Distribution Department, 486 Broadway, Suite 500E, New York, NY 10013; telephone, 212-925-0606; e-mail, ORDERS@WMM.COM. *Daughter Rite* copyright 1978 by Michelle Citron. *What You Take For Granted* . . . copyright 1983 by Michelle Citron.

Published by the University of Minnesota Press
111 Third Avenue South, Suite 290
Minneapolis, MN 55401-2520
http://www.upress.umn.edu

Library of Congress Cataloging-in-Publication Data

Citron, Michelle.
    Home movies and other necessary fictions / Michelle Citron
        p.   cm. — (Visible evidence ; v. 4)
    Includes bibliographic references (p.   ).
    ISBN 0-8166-3261-8 (hardcover : acid-free paper).—
    ISBN 0-8166-3262-6 (pbk. : acid-free paper)
        1. United States—Social life and customs—20th century—Fiction.
    2. Women authors, American—20th century—Family relationships.
    3. Citron, Michelle—Childhood and youth.   4. Family—United States—
    Fiction.   5. Domestic fiction, American.   I. Title.   II. Series.
PS3553.I866H66   1998
813'.5409—dc21   98-29233

Printed in the United States of America on acid-free paper

The University of Minnesota is an equal-opportunity educator and employer.

10 09 08 07 06 05 04 03 02 01 00 99 98   10 9 8 7 6 5 4 3 2 1

*for Edith, Sam, and Vicki
and Sue*

with love

Forty-three years old, and the war occurred half a lifetime ago, and yet the remembering makes it now. And sometimes remembering will lead to a story, which makes it forever. That's what stories are for. Stories are for joining the past to the future. Stories are for those late hours in the night when you can't remember how you got from where you were to where you are. Stories are for eternity, when memory is erased, when there is nothing to remember except the story.
:: Tim O'Brien, *The Things They Carried* (1990)

A book must be the ax for the frozen sea within us.
:: Franz Kafka, *Letter to Oskar Pollak* (1903)

Contents

Preface   XI

HOME MOVIES   I
    What's Wrong with This Picture?   2

AUTOBIOGRAPHY   27
    Speaking the Unspeakable: How We Talk When Words Fail   29
    The Simple Act of Seeing   53

NECESSARY FICTIONS   75
    The Story in 1988 . . .   77
    The Story in 1980 . . .   109
    The Story in 1969 . . .   115
    The Story in 1956 . . .   129
    The Story in 1997 . . .   137

ART   141
    Daughter Rite   143
    What You Take for Granted . . .   165

Acknowledgments   203

Notes   205

Selected Bibliography   209

Preface

The last story first. This is what happened.

Book done, I rubber-banded its printed pages into thick paper blocks and flew to see first my father, then my mother, who have lived at opposite ends of the country since their divorce over twenty years ago. I wanted to personally hand them the stories told here: scenes from our shared lives, and the secrets pried from beneath those scenes. These stories were their stories, too. Before they made their journey from the private space of the family into the public world at large, I thought it only right to ask my parents' permission.

An autobiographical work is intimately bound to the writer's psyche, a shadowy place where guilt and projection lurk. I feared my parents would seek to restrain me, to say, "No, you can't tell these things," or somehow worse, that they'd say nothing yet silently suffer a betrayal so deep that their love for me would fracture.

Apprehensive, I brought the manuscript to my father. Turned out, he was more nervous than me. Much to his relief, there were no new secrets lurking on its pages, no emotional ambushes, only the hard unfolding of truths already known. "It's wicked," he said. "Wicked." Much to my relief, he put his arms around me and smiled. "I respect you for writing it," he said. It was that, his respect, that did me in. I felt like an impostor. Had I really earned my father's respect? Writing had brought resolution to childhood experiences that had dominated my life in subtle and cunning ways. Despite my best intentions, there was little conscious volition in my selection of subject matter. As with much creative work, this book chose me; I just hung on for the ride.

Showing the book to my father was easy. Two weeks later I flew two thousand miles in the opposite direction to hand the manuscript to my mother. My anxiety in anticipating her reading generated enough energy to power the plane.

For three days my mother and I sat together at her dining room table and read: she the manuscript; me one of those distracting airport novels.

Picture this.

A dining room, or at least the feel of a dining room, created by the overly large French provincial table squashed into a corner of the tiny living room. The shifting mounds of curling newspapers, thumb-worn magazines, torn-out recipes, clipped grocery store coupons, and contest entry forms that usually blanket the table are swept to one side. In the small clearing at the end of the table my mother and I read, each hunched over her book, sharing the same physical space but inhabiting vastly different emotional terrains. The feelings that swirl around us are larger than any one room or time can hold. Anxiety and hope, anger and compassion, anguish and love, seep out of the present, infecting both the past and the future.

You write an autobiographical work caught in your real-life family entanglements. History, ambiguous and snaking, winds around the large and small decisions made every hour on the page. My mother sat next to me reading this book and I wondered: How had our ongoing relationship influenced the shape of my story? In what ways had entrenched emotional dynamics determined the truths told?

What tales were embellished larger than lived, turning the coward into the heroine, the mundane into the poetic? What stories were flattened or suppressed, coaxing love from my mother and father or, perhaps, the reader? I don't know. The censor, formed from the dazzling web of family dynamics, shifting emotions, and psychological defenses, blinds me to the distortions and absences on the page. Take those moments when I thought "this isn't important" and hit the delete key. Was the "this" really not all that important? Or was I just protecting my mother and father in the same way that, as a child, I protected them from the knowledge of my incest?

Are the silences in my autobiographical writing equivalent, in some real or metaphoric way, to the silences of my childhood? In the writing of this book did I unconsciously replicate my family's dynamics so that now, forty years later, I still protect them from certain kinds of knowledge? Do you never escape the repetition?

I hoped that my writing would break the pattern, that the words could hack me free from the compulsion to repeat. Who knows if I've succeeded? I can't even predict the stories, which if told, would break the set. They are like land mines buried in an overgrown field that I must walk through with my writing, whose location is known only by the explosion triggered by a verbal step. A leg is blown off, blood gushes out through the severed artery, and only then do I understand that what I've written exposes, maims, or kills. Despite our will and the best of intentions, the process of change is quite mysterious; often it is luck, coincidence, or the wily unconscious that converts.

And what about the acts of censorship of which I am conscious? In the battle between respecting the rights of my family and speaking the unspeakable, a conflict glibly defined as the right to privacy versus the right to know, where should I take my stand? Is it wrong to err on the side of caution? What is the value in exposing every single truth, or at least what I think is the truth, if it hurts or destroys? Whose purpose does it serve? My own? My parents'? The reader's? How do you sort through the competing motivations of narcissism, revenge, cowardice, and honesty?

As it turned out, my mother could have cared less about this tangle of issues. She had other concerns.

Imagine the mother and daughter sitting side by side, each lost in the world of her own reading.

The mother turns a page. The daughter steals a look without moving or otherwise signaling her curiosity. Another page flutters over. Then another. And another. The daughter finally turns a page of her own, although the time lapse since the last page turn has been so long, her mother must know she's only pretend-reading.

The mother looks up. Says nothing. The daughter leaps on the subtlest of signs. "What?" she asks.

The mother hesitates. "Do you . . . did you . . ."

"What?"

"The razor blades," says the mother, "did you . . . ah . . . you know . . . ah . . ."

"No," says the daughter. "I say that part's fiction." She thumbs through the pages until she finds the one she's looking for. "See," she says, pointing, "it clearly says that story is fiction."

The mother shrugs. "I guess so. But do you really think people will get it? Or care?" suggesting that the paper-thin line between imagination and experience is nonexistent, or perhaps irrelevant, in the mind of the reader.

Rats, thinks the daughter, the fiction, rather than reassuring my mother, confirms her worst fears of who I might be, what I might do. The daughter realizes that her mother, rather than seeing the interweaving of memoir with fiction as an elegant way to test the sly, fictitious nature of memoir against fiction's nugget of truth, accepts all the words as real. For the mother, her author-daughter owns everything she writes. Literally.

"How do you even think up such things?" asks the mother.

"Read books. Talk to people."

"It's confusing."

Defensive, the daughter launches. "I'm trying to do a lot of things here, Mom. Tell a good tale. Raise questions about memoir as a form of storytelling. Explore the line between fiction and lived experience. It's in the narrow current between the two that the truth breathes. It's at the border that we learn."

"Honey, that's awfully intellectual. Your educated friends might get it, but not average folks like me."

The daughter's struggle to create a form to walk the edge between the personal and the political, the psychological and the social, is irrelevant. The distinction between fiction and nonfiction is irrelevant. The differences in education between the mother and daughter create a chasm in which theoretical nuances are swallowed up by the sheer enormity of the distance. All the daughter can say is, "It's about the dance between memory and history. I'm trying to figure out a way to talk about experiences that are complex, confusing, contradictory, life changing. For me it was incest. But other experiences could be substituted."

"Like?"

"Any experience that is uncontrollable and terrifying and that overwhelms your ability to cope. A soldier who endures a horrific battle. A mindless, natural disaster that shatters everything you've built. Torture that breaks a prisoner's soul. Or the everyday, garden-variety tragedies of life: accidents, violence, illness, death."

"If it makes you happy, doll," says the mother and she goes back to reading.

The daughter watches another page turn. And another. The mother speaks without looking up, "I never knew Nana told you about her abortions. When did she do that?"

"When I went off to college. I think she was trying to warn me. She also told me to stay out of the tall grass with boys." They chuckle in chorus for a few notes, before the weight of their history muffles their fragile song.

Another page turns. And another. And another.

The mother looks up. "This is deep. Very deep." There is surprise laced with marvel in her voice.

Old habits die hard. The daughter avoids the real question—why are you surprised?—and takes the easy way out: "Is that good or bad?"

"Good. It's good."

The stack of pages gets smaller and smaller as the mother reads her way through the stories. At last only a few pages remain. The mother can't seem to turn them over, as though they weigh more than she can lift. She wipes the corner of one eye with a napkin-wrapped finger.

"Don't finish," her daughter says.

"I can't."

"Don't finish it. You already know what happens." The daughter reaches across the table and gently covers her mother's hand with her own.

For a held breath, the book slices through the fog that usually hangs between them; compassion and empathy slip through.

"I love you," says the mother.

"I love you, too," I say.

And so the story begins. Again.

Home Movies

*One looks at one's surrounding (and one is always
surrounded by the visible, even in dreams) and one
reads what is there, according to circumstances, in
different ways.*
::   John Berger, *Another Way of Telling* (1982)

What's Wrong

I watch a home-movie snippet shot by my father in 1956. It is a living moment, more than forty years old, fixed onto a slender thread of film: My mother holds my sister's and my hand as we walk away from and then toward the camera.

We move away, turn, then come closer to the viewer. In this one aspect only, it is the women of the family, and not my cameraman father, who are active. This sequence is actually made up of two shots: my father has chosen to stop the camera briefly when we turn around in the distance. Perhaps this moment does not interest him. More likely, he wanted to save film. This sequence is the next to the last one on the reel; he knew the film was running out. It is ten seconds long and was shot using a regular 8mm camera with a normal prime lens.

We parade up and down the sidewalk, for my father and the camera, in front of the apartment building where we lived. It is now expensive real estate. Forty years ago it was a waystop for working-class Jews fleeing from the poverty of inner-city Boston neighborhoods toward the suburbs of ranch houses and open lawns. My family never quite reached its middle-class goal, although this failure is inscribed in my memory and not in the image. What the image reveals is a mother and her two daughters, stylishly dressed in what I know were the clothes we wore to shul on the

with This Picture?

The Promenade

In 1888 a little camera called the Kodak allowed us to realize personal memories both inside the mind's eye and visible to the eyes of others. These memories were moments frozen in time, never-changing images of ourselves that we could revisit and show to our friends. Then in the twentieth century personal photographic memory began to move and flow: first with home movies and more recently with home video.

No matter how distinctive the technologies of still photography, motion pictures, and video may be—adding color, motion, sound, instantaneity— the images captured have remained surprisingly the same. As visual anthropologist Richard Chalfen has pointed out, changes in technology did not significantly change the images themselves; home moviemakers generally photographed the same things that snapshooters did.

We take billions of photographs and millions of hours of video yearly. Our lives are steeped in home images. These images spill out of photo albums,

High Holy Days of fall. These clothes say more about a time and place (fifties America, special occasion) than class; clothes for women can conceal economic status.

My sister and I sport matching pink outfits in the New Look: the full skirts and swinging A-line jackets of the prosperous postwar years. Dressed in these beautiful clothes made by my mother, we wear her optimism about the future on our backs. My mother herself hasn't quite made the transition out of the scarcity of the depression and the war. Her dark blue suit (also homemade) is a straight skirt number with a shoulder-padded jacket pinched at the waist. There is as yet no extravagant use of fabric in her clothes. Only her shoes—the impossibly high, pointed-toe heels of the fifties—hint at a different longing.

In my memory, my mother is overweight and often depressed, my sister is beautiful, and I am plain, if not ugly. The image, however, challenges this memory. My mother is beautiful, with the womanly figure fashionable at the time. My sister and I are both cute, if not downright pretty. But beyond surface appearance, there is an animated physicality, an energy, between us that brightens the screen. These people seem nice, warm, alive.

This ten-second image shimmers with the delight of possession: my mother of the clothes she made and the children who wore them, my father of his wife and daughters, the entire family of the camera that has occasioned this promenade.

As we walk toward the camera, my mother silently chats first to my sister, then to me. Forty years later I imagine her saying, "Stand up straight," or perhaps, "Smile." My sister doesn't quite understand the home-movie ritual and is more interested in my mother and her own feet. As we walk forward, my mother shakes my sister's hand for emphasis and nods toward the camera. My sister, so prompted, looks up and waves. "Bye-bye," she mouths.

I need no such coaching. In fact, I instruct. I coax my sister, point at the camera, and perform with assurance. I lean into the lens, pulling my mother and sister into close-up. I already understand the camera and have my own relationship to it. I am already a director. Only my mother's firm

sheboxes, wallets, desk tops, and bookshelves, reflecting our memories back to us: who we were, who we knew, what lives we lived.

The desire to capture these home images is, to a great extent, shaped by commerce. When *America's Funniest Home Videos* was first broadcast, camcorders, donated by manufacturers to ABC affiliates, were made available to viewers for test shoots. This stimulated home videomaking, thereby providing programming for the show.[1] People were further encouraged by the $10,000 prize awarded each week for the audience's favorite tape. Not surprisingly, in its second year of broadcasting *America's Funniest Home Videos* received two thousand tapes daily. At the same time, camcorder sales were up noticeably. An increased desire for home videos was created, selling cameras to consumers and audiences to advertisers.

This has always been the case. We became a nation of home-movie makers in the first place because of a massive marketing initiative. When Kodak developed 16mm motion picture film in 1921, they asked Marion Norris Gleason, a neighbor of one of the film's inventors, to write a short film to be used to publicize the new technology. The original home movie, *Picnic Party,* was of her son Charles's first birthday celebration. This film promoted the possibilities of the new technology to both company executives and the potential home market.[2]

By 1927 the United States had about half a million amateur moviemakers.[3] This technology was expensive. In 1932 Kodak's cheapest

grip on my hand reigns in my energy. But my bobbing head, swinging arms, and bouncy steps suggest that she can't quite contain me.

There is another way to interpret our actions. My three-year-old sister is still connected to the Mother. I am already moving toward the Father. Am I posing for the camera with my mugging and waving, or is it my father I'm smiling for? Does this image represent how I want to be seen, or how my father chose to see me? Is my attraction to my particular father, or to the power of the Father, expressed through my real father's ability to conduct this walk? By growing up to be a filmmaker, do I become the Father and thus ascend to a kind of power? Or do I want to become him simply because I desire to stand outside the scene—in the space of safety behind the glass wall of the lens, where I can't be touched?

One side of our faces is brightly lit, the other side lies deep in shadow: the sharp low-key lighting of either early morning or late day, the light of melodrama and film noir, the dark side of both soul and culture. This lighting is intensified by the film stock itself. The highly saturated Kodachrome reds and yellows have faded, leaving behind only shadowy, cool blues and greens. Ironically, and certainly unintentionally, this lighting hints at my remembered, as opposed to my photographed, family.

The year this image was filmed was a difficult one for me, though you can't see that in the moving image. In 1956, at age eight, I wanted so desperately to die that all I could think about was ways to kill myself: drink the bottle of cough syrup, chew up all the aspirin in the jar, run in front of a moving car. But paralyzed by an overwhelming fear of death and screams of terror in the night, I didn't do any of these things. Instead I became ill and was hospitalized on and off for a good part of the year. All of this is banished from the space of the image. The low-key lighting is due to the vagrancies of the available light; the dark colors are the result of the natural chemical deterioration of the film.

In my family, home movies were powerful and necessary fictions that allowed us to see and explore truths that could only be looked at obliquely. We'd gather in front of the large flickering images projected onto the living-room wall because to look directly at the tiny frames of the film would

motion-picture camera, a spring-wound 16mm with one prime lens, cost what an average hourly worker earned in two weeks. Three minutes of film and processing cost a day's labor. But in that same year regular 8mm film was introduced. It cost half as much as 16mm and made home movies financially accessible to working-class families.

Further technical accessibility came in 1965 with the introduction of Super 8. With its slip-in cartridge, battery-operated motor, zoom lens, and built-in light meter, Super 8 was a consumer-friendly camera that anyone could run. Now we have fully automatic video camcorders, around sixteen million in the United States, or about one for every six households.

We are bombarded with print advertisements and television commercials telling us to capture our memories on film and tape. Supermarkets sell film at the checkout counter, nudging you to buy that extra roll. Hotel lobbies, souvenir stores, and airport newsstands display throwaway cameras, just in case you've forgotten yours at home. Is it any surprise that vacationers take 70 percent of all photographs shot worldwide?

Advertisements for film, camera manuals, and even photo shop displays of the various enlargement sizes provide us with examples of what the "good" memory looks like: having fun on vacation, children with animals, families that play or celebrate together.[4] From the glossy surface of these home images slides the story of the happy family.

For the family is central to the images shown: the birth of a baby is one of the primary motivations reveal nothing. We'd stare at these grainy and subdued images, looking for their secrets, because to turn and peer into the lens of the projector would blind us. Home movies were our memory, anchoring us in time and perpetuating the fictions we needed to believe about ourselves.

Home moviemaking began in my family in 1947 when my father borrowed a regular 8mm camera to take with him on his honeymoon. Soon after, my father bought his own camera, which he continued to take movies with during the twenty-seven years of my parents' marriage, the first twenty-six years of my life.

In my family there were always home movies: shooting them and watching them. My father filmed birthday parties, holiday dinners, barbecues, Girl Scout picnics, couples' club outings. These, like our promenade for the camera, were public moments of family pride. My father, quite interestingly, also filmed many private and banal domestic events: my sister and I cleaning house, washing dishes, mending clothes, making the beds.

An integral part of the movies was their exhibition. Every few months, when we had nothing to do or had relatives visiting, the small reels came out of the shoeboxes, the screen and projector were set up, and an evening was spent watching ourselves. We all provided the live sound track.

Picture this. It's Sunday night, sometime in the early sixties. We've all just settled down to watch our home movies, adults on the sofa, children cross-legged on the floor. The lights are dimmed. The grainy and scratched image of an earlier time flickers on the wall:

The Birthday Party

INT. LIVING ROOM. DAY. 1952

The decor is a working-class fantasy of upper-class life: heavy, ornate furniture, gold-painted mirrors, porcelain figurines of chubby cherubs and court ladies. The room is packed with family—children, parents, grandparents, cousins, aunts—and playmates. At the center of all this activity, dressed in matching pink organdy dresses, are the two daughters—Michelle and her younger Sister, ages four and one.

for purchasing a camera. On *America's Funniest Home Videos* we see families everywhere: families on picnics, families on vacation, families at little league games, families at the mall. And kids are the heart of the family: in bathtubs, in kitchens, in backyards; scrubbing, eating, playing, splashing, spilling, slipping. On the surface everything is wholesome and cute, but a dark shadow of power bleeds through.

Susan Sontag writes in *On Photography* that "to photograph is to appropriate the thing photographed. It means putting oneself into a certain relation to the world that feels like knowledge—and, therefore, like power." Many of the tapes shown on *America's Funniest Home Videos* reveal that power by capturing the small humiliations of childhood: falling into your food, being caught on the toilet, dropping your pants. The embarrassments are even manufactured to create a more competitive video.

A mother, unable to stop her three-year-old daughter from interrupting her in the bath, threatens to disappear down the drain if her daughter won't behave. The mother sets up the camcorder, hides behind the shower curtain, and in a high, squeaky voice pretends to have been sucked down the drain. Predictably the child, panicked, cries into the drain, "I don't know what to do! Mommy, come out!" The audience laughs and applauds; the child is publicly disciplined. Though we all probably have at least one embarrassing childhood moment hidden away on a home-movie reel, in my imagination these moments have multiplied a thousand-fold as people scramble for the show's prize. The

As the image plays on the wall, WE HEAR OFF SCREEN the voice of the family in 1962—Mother, Grandmother, Grandfather, Michelle, Sister, and Dad—watching, commenting.

The CAMERA sweeps the room. Children crowd the table, the mothers and fathers hover behind them, making sure cake meets mouth. The CAMERA comes to rest on the birthday girl, the younger Sister. She puckers and blows out the candles.

DAD (V.O.): You were such a cute baby.
SISTER (V.O.): DAD!

The shaky CAMERA PANS up to Mom, cutting the cake.

MOTHER (V.O.): God, I've put on weight.
GRANDMOTHER (V.O.): No, you haven't.
MOTHER (V.O.): Look at me there.

The image suddenly shifts. Another birthday party. Michelle, the older daughter, holds up a cellophane-wrapped doll.

MOTHER (V.O.): Remember that toy?

Michelle grunts. The mother ignores her daughter's adolescent surliness.

MOTHER (V.O.): It was your favorite doll until the arms fell off. (*To no one in particular*) Who gave it to her?
GRANDMOTHER (V.O.): Cousin Ruth.

The CAMERA PANS the adults, clustered in the corner, smoking, schmoozing. At the center is the Grandmother.

MOTHER (V.O.): You look so young there.

Michelle, the birthday girl, wanders by. An adult reaches down and adjusts her party hat.

GRANDMOTHER (V.O.): You were always such a happy baby. Look, there's Sadie! She's dead now, *keyn eyn-ore*. God, she could make me laugh till I peed in my pants.

There is giggling as all remember.
Flicker. Change. The image of Michelle kissing her cousin fills the wall.

MOTHER (V.O.): You always loved your cousin.
GRANDFATHER (V.O.): (teasing) Yeah, kissing cousins.

The reel runs out, the wall flickers white. Silence . . .

The Party

visual memory of childhood is thus sold to the highest bidder.

Photographs are usually taken by parents of children. They represent the parents' memories, not the child's. Later the "children are offered a 'memory' of their own childhood, made up of images constructed entirely by others . . . one version of family history, which represses much lived experience."[5]

The camera freezes the child's life, which can then be stored for safekeeping in an album or a box or a tape. In home images the child never grows up, gets drunk, sleeps around, or breaks your heart. Deterioration and death are stopped, but so is the process of development and independence. At a deep-down level, these images may betray a parental panic of losing one's children.

Most often it is the father who holds the camera and peers through the lens. With still images, the mother often sorts and writes the narrative into the family album, providing another voice to the story; with moving images, however, Dad has near total control. With film in particular, positioned behind the lens, constrained by a roll of celluloid that lasts only three minutes, Dad must edit in the camera, constantly making choices of what to film. Even with videotape running up to two hours, decisions must be made: what to shoot, what focal length of the lens to use, how to frame the shot. Technology, as we all know, is historically the province of men. On *America's Funniest Home Videos,* the $10,000 prize winner is announced and the program's host, Bob Saget, approaches the family sitting in the audience. He kneels down and sticks the microphone in

Watching home movies together, providing live commentary, gave my family a sense of history of themselves as a unit and a way to position themselves in the past, where everyone was younger, thinner, healthier, happier, and together. This of course was not a real past, for only the younger part was true. We needed to believe that the visual "evidence" was honest (seeing is believing). We took the surface image as a sign for the whole lived experience. We wanted to believe that the piece was, in fact, the whole.

By watching the home movies in this way, retelling our story, my family created yet another level of necessary fiction, a fiction that could help us cope with older, deteriorating bodies in a less-than-ideal and fractured present. The home-movie images allowed us to believe that the sunny side of life did exist, if only in the past, and thus they gave meaning to otherwise difficult lives.

I like the silence of the home movies (unlike video, which has unceasing sound). There were moments in my childhood when I would lean against my grandmother's body, my head rising and falling with her breath, the warm smell of popcorn in the room, a salty taste on my tongue . . . and just listen. As I drifted in and out of sleep, adults filled up the silent space of the images with memories evoked: the joy of a moment well lived, the desolate pain of a death. The past tense of the images mingled with the present tense of the storytelling. For this brief space of timelessness I felt a part of something larger than myself; I was safe.

It is 1997. I thread up the projector: the 8mm reel of "The Birthday Party" filmed by my father in 1952. But times have changed. I'm watching it alone, my family members either scattered or dead. It is my turn to give the movies a present tense.

Now I can say that I see a large and happy Jewish family of the early fifties. It is a family where the children seem special. They are the center of attention. It is their birthday. The adults are always watching, primping, holding, giving, and the camera itself spends most of its time looking at them. Children are the family's pride and joy. There is love and safe harbor in the constant intermingling of generations, as seen, for example, in the image of my grandmother with her young grandson and granddaughter

Dad's face. "You were [the one] videotaping?" asks Bob. "I was, yes," says Dad. "Taking a guess here," says Bob with a shake of his head and a knowing smile.

Family home movies are filled with images of the girls—the mother, wife, or daughters—parading as objects in front of the father's gaze through the camera's eye. There are, of course, the occasional acts of rebellion: the mother sticks out her tongue, covers the lens with her hand, runs out of the frame. She attempts to resist the father's total control. In a filmic sense, this is a moment of the subject's power. The mother returns the gaze of the symbolic Father and defies it. But her action is playful and tame. We all know families have such tension; these moments do not threaten the real balance of power.

In home movies we often connect directly to the person behind the lens, a relationship found in portrait photography but rarely in commercial narrative film. Home movies represent how the person behind the camera chooses to film the way the person in front of the camera presents his or her "self." As cultural theorist Roland Barthes has written about the photographic image, "In front of the lens, I am at the same time: the one I think I am, the one I want others to think I am, the one the photographer thinks I am, and the one he makes use of to exhibit his art." With parents and children, husbands and wives, the image often reproduces the power dynamic existing outside the frame. The ubiquity of these home images, each resembling another, makes what they record seem natural. By (my cousins) leaning contentedly against her body. There is a lot of smiling. There is a lot of action: talking, eating, touching, playing. The birthday party looks busy and chaotic; this family is not quiet or repressed.

There is also gender differentiation. The little boys wear ties and look like men, while the little girls wear frilly, pastel dresses with round collars and full organdy skirts, presenting the innocence of girlie perfection. Everyone is dressed in his or her best, suggesting a distinction between work and leisure, public and private. And, there is the showing off of material gain. Hence how we look—what we wear, eat, carry, buy—is important. The adults pictured grew up in the depression, after all. The camera records plenty: plenty of food, plenty of decorations—special hats, plates, cups— plenty of gifts. As in the home movie of "The Promenade," these people seem proud of their possessions. The home movies offer a fiction of the family that reinforces what they want to know about themselves and sanctions a public view of a most private space: the home.

But I must add, when I've read my home movies with this ethnographic eye, it has always provided distance and protection for me: from the images themselves, the feelings they elicit, and the family they represent. By focusing on the social and deemphasizing the psychological, I have made the home movies safe.

When I asked my father for the home movies, my request was motivated less by ethnographic interest or sentimental longings and more by my anger about the absences: the grim fights over money (there was never enough), suffocating intrusiveness, emotional manipulations, and the rage, always the rage, I had felt as a child. These absences invalidated my memory and thus my feelings about my childhood, family, and self. I could not tolerate the conflict between the image truth and the memory truth.

I watched my family's home movies over and over, trying to understand why they didn't show what I remembered; why I felt a lie. This family seemed so nice, loving, normal. I was disturbed. I was obsessed. I kept trying to figure out why the images I saw flickering on the wall had no correspondence to the memories flickering in my mind. Sister, friends, strangers came over to my house for dinner. Little did they know there was a price to

providing the "good" memory, home movies show us an ideal image of the family with everyone in his or her proper place: parents in charge, men in control, families together.

Sometimes, however, the ideal family memory is used ironically. The film *Philadelphia* (1993) ends with a montage of romanticized home-movie images: a boy-child plays baseball, carries a Halloween pumpkin, builds sandcastles on the beach. These images of Andrew Becker (Tom Hanks) as a young child are seen on a television placed in the midst of the memorial gathering of his friends and family following his death from AIDS. These images evoke a more innocent time, not only for the character, but for a pre-AIDS, more sexually liberated America.

The home movies represent family warmth and normality for the boy-character who grows up gay and sympathetic in a film marketed for mainstream America. Going on a picnic, playing on the beach — these images look like the home movies we all have of our childhoods. We see that Andrew Becker was a child just as we were children; Becker is like us, we are like Becker. Our identification with the character, through the homogeneity of home-movie images, breaks down the otherness of homosexuality.

The point is driven home by our belief in the authenticity of these images, or at least a belief that what we see in the photograph must exist, or have existed, in order to be photographed.[6] As Roland Barthes has written, with the photograph, "the power of authentication exceeds the power of representation." Or, in the words of one of pay. For after dinner I would sit them down in the darkened living room and make them watch the home movies. What do you see? Does this seem like a happy family to you? Do you think all is as it seems to be? I badgered them with questions. I'm sure they thought me meshuggeneh, as my mother would say. But I had to understand the split between what I saw and what I remembered. This is why I made *Daughter Rite,* my fifth film: to reread the image of my family's home movies. To unpack the pictures, exposing the meaning I knew lay just beneath the surface appearance.

Daughter Rite is a faux documentary film of two adult sisters, Stephanie and Maggie, who have returned to their mother's home while she lies ill in the hospital. This "cinema verité" narrative thread, of the sisters talking about their relationship to their mother, is interwoven with a second family's story: that of an unnamed Narrator and her relationship with her sister and her mother. The Narrator speaks over home movies that have been optically printed to manipulate the images, often repeating a movement over and over again. The documentary footage is staged, scripted, and acted; the home-movie images have been processed with techniques developed by avant-garde filmmakers in the early seventies. Thus the film's aesthetic blurs the boundaries between documentary, narrative fiction, and experimental filmmaking. By doing so, it brings into relief yet another fiction: the separation between documentary, experimental, and narrative fiction film.

Daughter Rite is a movie of my family's home that incorporates my family's home movies, expressing what I *felt* when I watched them. Let me illustrate with two scenes from the film. One is a sequence where the Narrator relates a dream in which she was forced to take an injection she did not want. The second scene follows sequentially in the film. In this scene, Stephanie, one of the "documentary" sisters, looks directly into the lens of the camera and tells the story of being raped by her stepfather.

The dream sequence uses eight of the original forty shots filmed by my father in the home movie of "The Birthday Party." I've selected the most disturbing moments and refilmed them to investigate and present their implicit, rather than explicit, meanings.

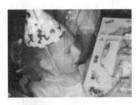

anthropologist Richard Chalfen's home-movie informants, "It's real if you've got a picture of it."

This is the intent behind the use of home-movie-like images in political commercials. Mark McKinnon, the media consultant who created 8mm political spots for Clair Sargent, the Democratic Senate nominee from Arizona in 1992, says he created false home movies designed to look like the real thing to "communicate a sense of reality and humanity about the candidate."[7] Despite their phoniness, the Sargent home movies signify, like all home movies, "authenticity": an objective recording of an actual event captured by the home-movie camera.

Film historian Patricia Erens analyzed the use of faux home-movie images in conventional narrative commercial films. Looking at such films as *Raging Bull, Peeping Tom, Unsuitable Job for a Woman, The Falcon and the Snowman,* and *Paris, Texas,* she found that the home-movie scenes were "coded as documentaries, images which . . . don't lie."[8] Even in experimental films, such as the work of avant-garde filmmakers Stan Brakhage, Ken Jacobs, and Jonas Mekas, the visual style of home movies is used to express the spontaneous, untampered nature of their own films.[9] But what exactly is real?

We are not naive. We know these images are staged. We've all been asked to pose in front of a famous landmark or file past the camera, waving as we look directly into the lens. With their moments of family members mugging at the lens and children's birthday parties that seem to exist only for the camera to record, home movies teeter at the

Slowed down and repeated, the images reveal another film that had been obscured at the normal speed. Under the scrutiny of slow motion, my mother repinning my hair becomes an agonizingly intrusive and possessive gesture; her helping me with a spoon becomes an invasion of my boundaries; her reaching for a gift blots me out. I am obviously very angry with my mother and see her as the source of my disturbed childhood. It is in this shadow film of the home movies that I believe my real family exists. It is in the nonverbal communication revealed through the image manipulation that a deeper meaning lay for me: a more profound family that cannot be hidden from the camera despite my father's focus.

In the second sequence, Stephanie's story of her rape, my film characters are talking heads, not whole bodies. Although Stephanie tells a traumatic body story, it is expressed through language and faces only. It's as if the bodies are too dangerous or shameful to be seen. She tells the moment; we do not see it. If the home movies are about behaviors, these "documentary" sequences of the film are about words. If the home movies are about moving, acting bodies, these "documentary" scenes are literally talking heads. Much of *Daughter Rite* uses talking heads, not bodies, as though the images of bodies cannot be trusted.

Daughter Rite strikes a chord with many women. I'm not sure why. At the time it came out I suspected it spoke to a dark secret that lay in many a daughter's heart: the anger we felt toward our mothers. An anger that needed to be seen in the larger patriarchal context I only alluded to in *Daughter Rite*. I screened the film in museums and festivals around the world: the Museum of Modern Art, the Whitney, the Walker, New York, Berlin, London, Edinburgh. I was not afraid of public presentation. But my mother was another story.

After I made *Daughter Rite,* I didn't show it to my mother for almost two years. When she finally saw it I cheated. I sliced out two scenes. I believed she would hate me if she saw those scenes, but I wasn't sure why. The scenes I cut were stories told to me by two of the thirty-five women I had interviewed in preparing the film. One was Stephanie's rape story. The other was a brief scene near the beginning of the film in which the

The Kiss

edge of both documentary and fiction. Herein lies a paradox: spontaneous *and* directed, authentic *and* constructed, documentary *and* fiction. This paradox is revealed every time we look at an image with which we have a personal relationship.

Kodak might have taught us how to film a vacation, but it is still *our* particular family's vacation that father shoots. On the surface of the home image, one family looks like any other: roughhousing on the beach, having a picnic, visiting the Statue of Liberty. Yet each of us has knowledge that cracks the smooth surface of our home images: a pending divorce, an alcoholic parent, an unemployed father, a depressed child. This information outside the frame is a constant reminder that home movies are highly selective in what they show.

We film Christmas dinner with family and friends, not the meal eaten alone; birthday parties, not the emergency room visits; baby's first step, not fighting with the adolescent; vacation, not work; wedding parties, not divorce proceedings; births, not funerals. Through our selective filming, the "sunny side of life" is preserved and the dark side of life is cast out.[10] We record the noteworthy, the celebrated, the remarkable, and the extraordinary.[11] Or perhaps their memorialization on film codifies these events as such.

In presenting the image of an ideal selective past, home movies announce what is absent. They stand in for what is there *and* what is not there. In their ambivalence they both confess and hide. The home movies are simultaneously acts of self-revelation, self-deception, and self-conception.

Narrator-daughter speaks of her mother's denial about her own (the mother's) debilitating depression. Neither scene was autobiographical. But I was overwhelmed with guilt and anxiety about the secret the film spoke—a daughter's anger—and somehow I thought that without these two scenes I could fool my mother about the depth of my rage. I was so emotionally overwrought when my mother saw even this edited version that I burst into tears before the opening credits. Being a good mother, she stroked my hand and told me everything was going to be fine. I had conveniently shifted the emphasis of the viewing from her reactions and feelings to mine.

Daughter Rite was a story I constructed but could not read. But my mother could and did. Here is what eventually happened. Two years after I showed my mother the abridged edition, I was invited to show *Daughter Rite* at the art museum in the city where she lived. She was excited. She planned a party for me afterward and invited all her friends. I was, of course, terrified. The day of the screening I ate almost two pounds of crystallized fruit—pure sugar—and proceeded to get very sick. This was uncharacteristic. I stood outside my body and watched myself abuse it. I was astounded. I knew my behavior was a sign of a deep disturbance, but I couldn't name it, nor could I stop myself.

The day after the screening my mother and I went for a walk. She said she wanted to tell me something disturbing, but she knew I could handle it. The sun was shining. The hibiscus swayed in the trade-wind breezes. I smiled at her, nodding my head with encouragement. Inside I was silently screaming, "No, shut up! I don't want to know!" But I kept smiling and nodding and so my mother told me: how she was sexually abused by her brother from the time she was eight until she was twelve. How he would sneak into her room at night, tie her to the bed, and rape her. As he left he would say, "If you ever tell anyone about this, I'll kill you. Even when you're grown up I'll come after you and get you." I am the first person my mother ever told this secret to; she was sixty-four years old when she told me, the day after seeing *Daughter Rite.* I think she believed that if I could make *Daughter Rite,* I could hear her secret. And she was right.

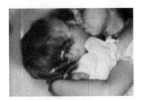

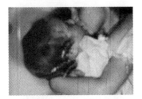

I receive a Christmas photo card from a friend. The image shows him, his partner, and their four children, dressed in matching outfits—black trousers or black skirts with bright red turtleneck sweaters—posed for the camera. The card is like many I receive, except that both parents are male. This image startles. Shot in a studio, floating against a white backdrop, my friend's "family," unlike the families in the other Christmas photographs I'm sent, is disconnected from the environment in which they live. The card at once parodies the suburban nuclear family they are outside of *and* calls it forth to legitimize themselves and their children. Being both gay and a parent is an experience that allows my friend to appropriate the typical Kodak family Christmas image when he creates his own.[12]

I agree with art critic John Berger when he writes in *About Looking* that "photographs . . . [and I would include home movies] in themselves do not narrate. . . . The private photograph . . . remains surrounded by the meaning from which it was severed . . . a memento from a life being lived."

Personal home images are fetishes. In the Freudian sense of the term, the home movie is counterphobic: a device that avows and disavows in the same sequence. The home movie opens a potential space where we can enter either its affirmations or its silences. What we experience in this ambiguity is determined at the moment of reading.

Parents express their displeasure at errant children by taking their high school portraits off the wall. People vent their anger at divorced spouses by

This moment of secret sharing changed forever my relationship to my mother: I understood the enigma of my childhood and my rage, misdirected in its exclusivity toward her. This moment changed forever my relationship to myself: my mother's telling me about her incest broke apart my own life and forced me to finally come to terms with my own experience of incest with my grandfather. This moment changed forever the meaning of the home movies. I had read my family's narrative in the home movies. I had appropriated the medium that was complicit in preserving the idyllic vision of the family, though I was unconscious of what I was doing at the time. And my mother had read my film back to me. As a family, we finally remembered and started to understand and speak our secrets.

In home movies we look directly into the lens, a filmic moment rare, even for documentaries. In home movies the gaze of the subject meets the gaze of the spectator. When I look at my family's home movies, my forty-eight-year-old self and my eight-year-old self meet each other's gaze across the gap of decades. I wonder what she will speak.

I go back to the home movies. I sift through the images, looking for evidence of my abuse. A clue. A visual symptom. Freud said the repressed always returns. Trauma always leaves a trail, if only you know how to read the markings. I want to find evidence of the incest secreted in the behaviors I see on the screen.

There is a sequence that arrests me. By the time this bit of film was shot, I was already experiencing ongoing sexual abuse. I am six years old, my sister is three. We are in our pajamas: frilly baby dolls that make us look like baby Lolitas, curlers that bestow a poignant vulnerability.

I pull my sister toward me, place her arms around my neck, and hold her tight against my body as I kiss her. Repeatedly, I kiss her long and hard on the mouth. I don't know how she reacts in this first shot because the camera discreetly, or so it seems to me, tilts down to give us privacy. There is an ellipsis. In the second shot I scoop my sister into a bear hug. She tries to pull away. I reach down and grab her ass and hold her to me. She struggles and squirms out of my grip. She beats her little fists against my chest, her face scrunched up with tears. I react by jumping up and down while

slashing their images out of the frames. Out of sight, out of mind. Gone. A grandiose power over life and death.

When a friend's house was threatened by fire, all she took was two suitcases: one filled with clean clothes and toiletries, the other jammed tight with photographs of her recently deceased brother. She felt deeply about these images: their iconic nature made them sacred.

When someone dies and fades from memory, you can look at a photograph and lived moments with that person burst into your mind: a secret shared, a heart-stopping betrayal, a mysteriously intimate moment. Perhaps that is why it was once fashionable among immigrant families to have a photograph of the deceased enameled onto the gravestone, a device both literal and symbolic, profane and sacred.

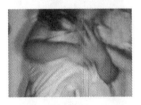

Historian Michael Lesy writes that snapshots (and I would include all home images) "are primarily psychological documents. They may be understood aesthetically, anthropologically, and historically as well. But . . . because they are personally and privately made images whose information is graphic, tacit, factual, and allusive, they must first be deciphered as if they were dreams." Like all dreams they hold the promise of both insight and terror. In the image, we confront what we both long for and deny.

The meaning of home images is in constant flux. This is due, in part, to the fact that we provide a second track, either stories or memories, at the moment of viewing. By doing so we fuse the

I laugh at the camera. My parents, or at least my father, who was looking through the lens of the camera, watched me manhandle my sister and saw nothing of what I see now. He kept filming, so he probably thought we were being cute.

I find my behavior aggressive, dominating, and disturbingly sexual. And though hints of this type of behavior exist in earlier home-movie clips, this strip of film is the first moment where they coalesce into an obscene parody of male dominance. I want to attribute this filmic moment to the incest: an acting out on my sister of the sins of my grandfather, a displaced sexual aggression forced onto a child younger, smaller, and more helpless than myself. I am mean and corrupted and I laugh. I seem thrilled by the coupling of sexuality and power. In the harsh, flat glare of the camera's floodlights, the film is profoundly disturbing. This image breaks my heart.

If in the home-movie clip of "The Promenade" I want to identify with the Father behind the camera, in this fragment of film my desire is fulfilled. I become the Father in all his grotesqueness. I did not know for what I wished.

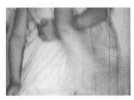

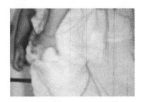

present tense of viewing to the past tense of recording. Time folds back on itself. Two places on the time line of our life meet. In this moment of superimposition, a space is created from which insight can arise. This is the latent hope in all home movies.

In my family, my mother expressed her defiance by sticking out her tongue at my father's camera eye. She expressed her anger toward the institution of the Father by pulling her own father's photographs off the wall and hiding them. I grew up, formed by feminist politics and the study of film, to take the means of producing the visual memory of the family away from the Father. If I had daughters, I am sure, they would tell a different tale.

Autobiography

"Hey," I said, "When you, do you sort of make it up, or is it just, you know, like what happens?"

"Neither."

:: Martin Amis, *Money* (1984)

Speaking the Unspeakable:
How We Talk When Words Fail

In our search for meaning we make symptoms, trouble, and art.
:: Robert Romanyshyn

A memory fragment. My father towel-dries my wet hair on a wintry night, the strong kneading of his fingers against my scalp—physical, intimate, safe.

Another memory fragment. I lay down beside my good grandfather, Abraham, my father's father, for our Saturday afternoon nap. He sleeps, softly snoring. I rest against his broad wall of a back, lifting and dropping with the rhythm of his breath, intently coloring the shapes in my book with blue and yellow crayons, innocent and bright. Later when he awakes I curl in his soft lap as he gazes over my head at the round, black-and-white television perched high on his bureau, where two tiny, out-of-focus men punch each other over and over in the boxing ring.

For a long time there were no stories.

A film image. A solitary woman stands in her bedroom and plays the violin. The shot is in medium close-up: the woman from her waist up, the instrument tucked under her chin, her elbow arcing as she bows the strings. We can see only a fragment of the room in which she stands: a corner of a mirror draped with necklaces and scarves, the bureau top cluttered with bracelets and rings, bottles of perfumes and lotions. The young woman, she is perhaps twenty, plays Schönberg's Phantasy, op. 47, cool and intellectual, the dissonance restraining the emotional passion that almost, but not quite, breaks through. The music's atonality carries the promise of a melody, but it's just that, a narrative tease that remains unfulfilled.

Another film image. A woman dressed in a red coat walks into a house. The camera gazes down on her from a second-story porch. Dusk swallows light; the woman is a slash of red moving obliquely through the dark space of the frame. Who is this woman? Where is she coming from?

Has she just parted from her lover? Or does he wait for her in the house? Maybe it is her children who will greet her with hugs and laughter. The image, like Schönberg's hint of a melody, teases us with a story it never delivers. This image, from *Daughter Rite,* speaks clearly of longing and loss, yet remains narratively silent.

My experimental films were built from many such images, which expressed a range of emotions—passion, pain, joy, rage, wonder—but not who, what, where, when, or how. These were eloquent images yet inchoate, full of meaning yet narratively mute. As was I, unable to speak about the pivotal experience of my childhood—the trauma of incest at the hands, and body, of my maternal grandfather.

Why couldn't I tell the story of my incest? As Paul Fussell said about another brutal experience, World War I combat, the English language is perfectly adequate in its ability to describe such atrocities:

> . . . it is rich in terms like blood, terror, agony, madness, shit, cruelty, murder, sell-out, hoax, as well as phrases like legs blown off, intestines gushing out over his hands, screaming all night, bleeding to death from the rectum, and the like . . .[1]

Incest, too, can be described. We have words like fondling, penetration, sexual abuse, molestation, and rape. We also have the words of women who have experienced incest: "the sound of my father's zipper coming down";[2] "I woke with my father's penis in my mouth"; "blood and vomit all over the sheets"; "he forces me to eat it."[3]

So if incest can be described, what's the problem? Regarding war, Fussell maintains that the obstacle is the social one of "gentility and optimism . . . less a problem of linguistics than of rhetoric. . . . What listener wants to be torn and shaken [out of his complacency and ideology] when he doesn't have to be? We have made *unspeakable* mean indescribable: it really means *nasty*" (emphasis in original).

Incest is nasty. It is also incomprehensible. To understand incest requires us to tolerate contradictions and paradoxes that create psychological unease, even pain. There are many examples: an adult you intensely love and trust hurts you more than you can almost bear; a mother must choose between a child and a husband; a child's body betrays her with sexual arousal at the same time her sense of self is being shattered. Incest ruptures the tidiness of our world, betraying our belief in how things should be. No wonder talking about it disquiets us. But it is precisely this discomfort that clarifies the paradoxes we all, whatever our experiences, must come to terms with in our lives.

Incest gives us a window onto experiences we all have: how the mind works, how the way we are treated as children influences our development, how we integrate difficult experiences, and how we ultimately communicate in a myriad of subtle ways. With incest, the particularity of experience and the metaphoric meaning coexist.

Incest is an assault on the soul played out on the body and so often it is the body that speaks first. Because incest is such an intensely disorienting experience, children often don't remember it—one study showed that 20 percent of incest victims were amnesiac about the abuse.[4] Even when a child does remember, it is hard to communicate an experience surrounded with threats to ensure its secrecy. Threats that range from "Let this just be our special secret" to "If you tell anyone I'll kill you" to actually killing the child's pet as an object lesson in who's the boss. But as Judith Herman reminds us in her book *Trauma and Recovery,* "folk wisdom is filled with ghosts who refuse to rest in their graves until their stories are told." The truth will out. And the body is the unavoidable voice for such truths. It is eloquent in its ability to communicate the intensity of feelings surrounding incest. But it is difficult to hear, this voice of the body, because it is so honest and visceral. As Tim O'Brien writes in his book *The Things They Carried* about the trauma of combat, "A true war story, if truly told, makes the stomach believe."

The fiction that is about to unfold is called *Pandora.* It tells the story of the two Doras, whom I think of as the Dora-of-the-Mind and the Dora-of-the-Body, two aspects of the same character, representing alternative personas and strategies for moving through the world. Dora I confronts the unexplained and fearsome with her intellect; she analyzes, rationalizes, describes. In this way she tries to control the unruly. Dora II succumbs to her untidy desires; she acts. Yet this division is just a writer's convenience; the separation is reductive, the border is permeable and cannot hold.

The two Doras can also be read as the same character at two points in time. Dora I has mind-memory and the distance of its past tense. Dora II's memory resides in her body. Like the flashback, her tale from the past is told in the present tense. But even this division is false. Frequently with memory about a trauma, two points on the time line of our life meet. The memory-of-the-mind and the memory-of-the-body converge at a place that is both/neither past and/nor present. At this moment the image and the narrative struggle to become one.

DORA I: *I never had enough time. I gulped down my coffee in the morning while I scanned the New York Times and hurried off to my job—teaching young children to speak. I worked out at the gym on my lunch hour three times a week, had dinner with my best friend, Rosie, twice a*

week, and made love with my boyfriend, Joe, every Saturday night.
This was my life. Busy. Tidy. Reasonable. Except for one thing.

DORA II: *I wake in the dead hours of the night. Quietly slipping out of*
bed, so as not to wake Joe, I tiptoe into the bathroom, close the door,
and turn on the light. I gaze at myself in the mirror. Time stands still.
I feel such sorrow I can only rend my body in grief.

 I reach into the medicine cabinet and take out a razor blade. Star-
ing at my reflection I gently draw the blade across my skin, making the
most delicate of incisions. My cutting scares me, makes me almost
breathless, but I cannot stop. What scares me even more is that I don't
understand why nightly I draw the blade across my flesh, watching the
blood bead up through the split skin.

DORA I: *I'd cut only inconspicuous places—the tender underside of my*
upper arm, my inner thigh. Joe rarely noticed. When he did, I lied.

DORA II: *"Oh I must have scratched myself with a pin," I say. I tell no*
one what I do. I feel only shame.

 I read everything I can find on the subject, desperate to understand
this disturbing compulsion. Delicate self-cutting. That's what the litera-
ture calls it. I'm very good at research, but the books tell me nothing.

DORA I: *This is what my intuition told me. My body is an enclosed*
space. By cutting I hoped to carve a small keyhole between the inside
and the outside—the psychic space of my anxiety that held the secret
and my conscious mind that wanted so desperately to know. I yearned
for my secret to seep through the skin's opening with my blood.

 Only later, much later, did I remember my daddy tying me down in
the small bed and pushing his body into mine. Only then did I stop the
delicate self-cutting. But I haven't remembered this yet.

Frequently in trauma, the story of what happened surfaces not as a
verbal narrative, but as a symptom. This is particularly true when the
abuse happens to a child, still developing and forming her psychological,
social, and moral world; a child unable to comprehend or contextualize the
experience within an adult's system of thought.

 The meaning of such symptoms has been understood since the 1890s,
when Freud, Pierre Janet, and Joseph Breuer treated women suffering from
hysteria. They came to understand that hysteria was caused by the psychological impact of real trauma and that its symptoms were disguised expres-
sions of that trauma. Breuer and Freud's famous summation says it all:
"Hysterics suffer mainly from reminiscences."

Symptoms are signs that can be read. They are communications of the body that bypass words and consciousness. It was Freud who hypothesized what was being communicated—information concerning childhood sexual assault, abuse, and incest. But his theory was too disturbing. As has been well argued elsewhere, the implications of his work—the widespread sexual abuse of children from respectable middle-class families—couldn't be tolerated by Freud or the medical status quo. His work was met with silence. No one wanted to hear what he had to say. Freud reinterpreted the case studies into a theory of the unconscious that reread the symptoms not as signs of real sexual trauma, but as signs of repressed fantasies and desires. This idea became one of the cornerstones of classic psychoanalytic theory. Whether you believe Freud replaced the external reality of incest with the psychic reality of fantasy, or just expanded his ideas to include the psychic reality, the social consequences were the same.[5] Actual incest was denied; fantasy, much easier to tolerate than the possibility of such widespread incest, was accepted. Dora was, in fact, the name of the patient of Freud's on whom this moment of rereading the sign pivots.

DORA I: *One day I met Peter, the father of one of my students. There was a blizzard and he offered me a ride home through the mounting snow. I watched as he knelt in front of his daughter, buttoning her coat, tugging her knitted cap down over her ears against the bitter wind. A simple fatherly gesture. It thawed a frozen place in my heart that I didn't even know existed. One hour later Peter and I were having sex in my bed.*

DORA II: *What am I doing? I must be crazy. I have to tell someone so I call Rosie. "I hope you used rubbers," Rosie says. I immediately regret the phone call. I tell her that doesn't even deserve a response. "You're not going to see him again, are you?" she asks.*

I'm very definite. "Of course not. He's the father of one of my students. And even though he's separated from his wife, he's still married. The ethics here are questionable."

"Good," says Rosie.

DORA I: *But I didn't stop. I just split myself in two: friend and lover, Joe and Peter, work and sex, day and night, truth and lies. I had it all under control. I thought. One night I was having dinner with Rosie in your typical downtown, upscale, postmodern restaurant. As the plate of thinly sliced beef carefully draped over crossed leaves of endive capped with a pale mound of shaved radish was placed in front of me—*

DORA II: —*I look up. Across the room sits Peter and a beautiful woman, his wife. Their heads bend toward each other in quiet conversation, their fingers touch.*

DORA I: *I thought I was going to choke on my dinner.*

DORA II: *I show up at Peter's apartment. I sink into the couch as far away from him as possible. In silence Peter pours a splash of scotch into a glass and offers it to me. I shake my head no. Shrugging, Peter swallows it.*
   "I thought you were separated," I say. He tells me he is.
   "You looked awfully intimate in that restaurant," I say to him and get up to pour my own drink.
   He makes the usual apologies. He tries to be conciliatory. "Don't be angry," he tells me.
   "I'm not. I'm not a jealous person."
   "Oh, right," he counters.
   "Yeah," I say, "just like you're not married anymore."
   "You want to hit me?" Peter asks.

DORA I: *For a brief moment I almost did.*

DORA II: *"Don't be ridiculous."*
   Peter walks over and stands calmly in front of me. He takes the drink from my hand and sets it on the table. "Slap me," he says.
   "No."
   "Why? Because nice girls don't and you're a nice girl?"

DORA I: *Before I could think, before I knew what my hand was doing, I smacked him in the face with my open palm.*

DORA II: *"Harder," says Peter.*
   I hesitate a moment, then hit him again.
   "Harder."
   I hit again.
   "Harder."
   I hit him with all my strength. And grabbing his hair, tugging his head back, I kiss him intensely. Peter takes my shoulders and pushes me against the wall, pressing his body hard against mine. I give in to his strength for the briefest of moments, then fight back.
   Peter smiles and offers me the most tender of kisses. I melt into his arms.

To talk about incest is to air society's dirty linen in public. It embarrasses everyone. It upsets the social order by destroying the boundary that usually separates the experiences of the private sphere from the responsibilities of the public sphere. To talk about incest is to use communication to carry the psychological world into the social world. To talk about incest threatens the categories on which our entire social order is founded. No wonder denial and silence surround the issue. No wonder Freud retreated. Incest appears now because there is a political context—feminism—that abrogates the social amnesia and makes speaking possible.[6] However, we long to stuff incest under the bed along with the other dirty sheets. And we still do so by ostracizing it to the tabloid television talk shows, tacky tell-all books, or the privacy of the therapist's office, a kind of highbrow concealment.

One acceptable form of speaking is statistics. Here's an example. In the United States, one fifth of all women experience incest before the age of eighteen, and one woman in three experiences sexual abuse.[7] Somewhere between 2½ and 16 percent of men in this country experience sexual abuse as children.[8] I want to bring the statistics home. Look around your life, at the people you know. Odds are that many of them have an intimate knowledge of sexual abuse, as I myself have. See, we can personalize numbers. But usually numbers are used to politicize issues. They reveal patterns, confronting us with the enormity of the problem. In so doing, they paradoxically make the experience bearable. It is easier to cite numbers than to understand the overwhelming trauma of incest. Numbers, as shocking as they are, tidy up the experience. In their abstraction they distance, they make safe.

DORA I: *I fell asleep, my head nestled in the hollow of Peter's back. I had a dream.*

I am a young child holding on tight to my daddy's hand. We stand in front of a large brick building. "I want to show you my elephant," my daddy says.

DORA II: *I don't want to look.*

DORA I: *"Don't worry," my daddy says, "it's okay."*

DORA II: *I'm scared to look, but curious, too. I push the door open and peek inside. I see the elephant—gray and huge. I step inside the space still holding on tight to my daddy's hand. I stand very still. The elephant walks up to me and gently pushes its trunk between my legs.*

DORA I: *"See," says my daddy smiling down at me, "it's not so scary."*

DORA II: *See, it's not so scary.*

DORA I: *I awoke with a shrill pain that filled the space between my legs.*

DORA II: *Quickly I slip out of bed being careful not to wake Peter. Going into the living room, I grab my purse off the couch. With trembling fingers I unzip my bag and claw through it. I can't find what I'm looking for. Panicked, I dump the contents onto the carpet and shuffle through the items, finally grabbing at the small, thin plastic box. With trembling fingers I pry it open. A razor blade rests inside. I reach out to touch it; my hand hovers in the air. I take a deep breath. I will myself not to pick up the razor. It is the hardest thing I've ever done. Nervously my eyes dart around the room. The wall in front of me is solid glass, floor to ceiling, looking out high above the city. I push my open hand hard against it and watch as my fingers turn white from the pressure. It looks so small and vulnerable. Like a child's hand.*

And then I remember my dream.

DORA I: *I stared out past my reflection in the glass to the lake far, far below. It's not true, I told myself.*

DORA II: *It's not true. It can't be true.*

To speak beyond symptoms, first we must remember.

When we use the word memory, we usually mean explicit memory, what we commonly experience as normal recall, declarative and conscious. Explicit memory is hypothesized to be an actively constructed narrative built from an interplay between a few important details and the feelings attached to the event.[9] This memory is continuous, storylike and easily verbalized. Here, for example, is my memory of my first movie experience.

I was five years old and my father took me to see *Pinocchio*. When the evil Stromboli lured Pinocchio into the cage and locked him up, I was terrified. I started screaming at the top of my lungs in this huge, Saturday-matinee theater. My father leaned over, took my hand and led me into the bright sunny day. When we reached the sidewalk I felt protected, safe, the fear locked securely back inside the dark movie theater.

Traumatic memory, on the other hand, is not like ordinary memory. It does not have the fluidity of telling a story about a moment from childhood, or what happened yesterday. Instead, it is fragmented, emotional, inarticulate. This type of memory is called implicit memory.

If explicit memory is like a movie, traumatic, nonverbal implicit memory is like a single frame snipped out of the film: an inexplicable reaction to a smell, a kinesthetic feeling that can't be connected to an image, an image that can't be positioned within a narrative. This is what most people mean when they use the term flashback.

In *The Courage to Heal,* for example, one of the most popular books about incest, a woman remembers her rape in fragments, unconnected visual images searching for a narrative:

> I'd start having flashes of things—just segments, like bloody sheets, or taking a bath, or throwing away my nightgown. For a long time, I remembered all the things around being raped, but not the rape itself.[10]

Trauma memories are details from a past experience that, unlike explicit memories, can't be constructed into a narrative, either because the details can't be anchored by a feeling or because the feeling, too overwhelming, short circuits the process. There is evidence to suggest that this feature of traumatic memory is actually caused by changes in the central nervous system that occur during moments of trauma.[11]

Physically, trauma triggers a state of hyperarousal, what we learned in high school biology as the fight or flight response. This is actually a massive firing of the autonomic nervous system, which brings with it the release of neurochemicals that prepare the body to defend itself or flee. The response affects all aspects of the person—physical, emotional, cognitive—as well as the interactions among these functions. In a traumatic experience, not only is everything put on red alert, but knowledge, emotions, and memory, normally integrated, are cut off from one another.[12] This severing is functional. It protects the child, enabling her to get away psychologically when she can't escape physically. It is an altered state that allows her to leave her body in order to evade unbearable feelings. Janet labeled it "dissociation."

This is the language of science. Let me juxtapose it with the language of experience.

When novelist Sylvia Fraser first remembered her incest, it was her body that held the memory, unconnected to images, words, or narrative. Her disassociation from the experience was so extreme, her only route back was through her body. Here is her description of her first adult memory of her childhood abuse:

> Inside my apartment, I throw down my keys, lie on my bed, close my eyes, fold my hands . . . waiting. Spasms pass through me, powerful, involuntary—my pelvis contracts leaving my legs limp. My shoulders scrunch up to my ears, my arms press against my sides with the wrists flung out like chicken wings, my head bends back so far I fear my neck will snap, my jaws open wider than possible and I start to gag and sob, unable to close my mouth—lockjaw in reverse. These spasms do not feel random. They are the convulsions of a child being raped through the mouth.[13]

DORA I: *If Joe was the comfortable man, easily read in the flat light of day, Peter was the shadow rising up from the dark dream of my soul,*

thrilling and dangerous. I felt awake and alive in a way I had never be-
fore experienced. I had a right to this, I told myself . . . The truth was,
I couldn't stop.

DORA II: *Peter and I sit in the candlelight, the remains of dinner on the*
table between us.

　　"Do you like being scared?" Peter asks.

　　"Define scared," I say. "Roller-coaster scared or trapped-in-an-
elevator-with-a-crazy-man-holding-a-gun-on-me scared?"

　　"Roller coaster," says Peter.

　　"I don't know," I say.

　　"But what if you knew you would be safe, absolutely safe?" insists
Peter. "Would you surrender to the fear?"

　　"Is this a rhetorical question?"

　　Peter is not smiling. "Could you scare me?" he asks.

　　My stomach tightens, "Do you trust me?"

　　"Yes," he says.

　　"I could scare you."

　　"Do it," he says.

DORA I: *I searched Peter's eyes. Something had changed; this was a dif-*
ferent game that both thrilled and terrified me.

DORA II: *Peter walks away into the living room. I follow him. I place a*
chair in the center of the room.

　　"Sit down," I tell him. Peter says, "Make me."

　　"I don't have to make you," I tell him. "You want to."

DORA I: *The words tumbled out from a place deep inside, hidden even*
from me. Our eyes locked. I felt like a bully. It was exhilarating.

DORA II: *Peter drops his eyes. He sits in the chair and I bind his hands*
behind his back with his tie. I open my purse and take out the small,
thin plastic box. I remove the razor blade. Peter watches wordlessly.
I hold the razor in front of his face. "Is this for you or for me?" Peter
cannot speak. "Are you scared?" I ask him. His eyes widen. "Follow
me to my dark places," I whisper. "Trust me. I won't hurt you."

　　I slowly open the front of my shirt. Delicately I draw the blade
through my flesh above my breast. The cut is so fine, so shallow, that no
blood is drawn; the path of the blade is marked by only a thin translu-
cent line. I hold the bare blade in front of Peter's face.

　　"Yes or no?" I ask him. I look down between his legs. "Yes, I
think." I gently stroke my open palm across Peter's chest. "It won't

hurt," I say. "Look me in the eye. Do you want to be cut?" Breathless, Peter can only nod—yes.

"Say it."

He whispers, "Yes."

I lay the blade on his flesh. The incision is delicate, only a few frag-ile red beads. Peter moans. I kiss him deeply. I throw one leg over him, then the other, straddling his lap. I reach behind and untie his hands . . . I ask for one more thing.

DORA I: *And he gave it to me.*

Later I lay in bed, my head on Peter's chest, floating on his heart-beat. "Tell me something from your childhood," Peter said.

DORA II: *"There's nothing to tell."*

DORA I: *"What? No stories? I don't believe that."*

DORA II: *"Believe it."*

DORA I: *Peter had stepped over some line, so I shut down. He tried to reconnect. "Okay. I believe you," he said, "temporarily. I'll tell you a story from my childhood then. My father was a tall man. Over six feet. One day we were at the beach and he picked me up and carried me into the ocean in his arms. When the water was up to his chest my father lifted me above his head and threw me in. I was floundering in the waves, gulping down water and he yelled at me, 'Swim or you'll drown.' I hated him."*

DORA II: *"Did you learn to swim?"*

DORA I: *"Yeah," he laughed. "I was state champion."*

DORA II: *Peter's fingertips brush across a thin wound on my arm.*

DORA I: *"Did you do that to yourself?" he asked. "Cut yourself?"*

DORA II: *"Yes."*

DORA I: *I had never told anyone before.*

DORA II: *I am very scared.*

Reenactment is yet another way to speak. It is a story from the past played out in the present but in disguised form. As such, the reenactment simultaneously reveals and obscures. If you know the original story, the present behavior and actions make a kind of sense. But often you don't know the original story. Then you rationalize the behavior to mask the intuition you have that you're not in control. You feel possessed by demons but don't acknowledge that they're yours. Dora said, "I had a right to this . . . The truth was I couldn't stop."

Freud called reenactments of traumatic experiences "repetition compulsion." He saw these behaviors as attempts to master the traumatic event. But he ultimately viewed the attempts pessimistically, as a kind of hopeless wheel spinning. More recent psychological theory is kinder. Reenactments are seen cognitively as a possible replaying of the script to change the ending, or affectively as a reexperiencing of the emotions in an attempt to integrate them.[14]

Think of it this way. A reenactment is a script that you write and direct in order to recreate the relationship and dynamics of the traumatic moment. For this to work, you need transference: finding and casting the right person to play the part. Dora casts Peter. In him she finds a man with whom she feels safe enough to act out elements of her past experiences in an effort to resolve them. With Peter, she gets to play out the script of her incestuous relationship with her father without being dominated or controlled as in her childhood experience.

The reenactment is not a duplication of the original event. Rather, it is a detail from that event elaborated into a story, a narrative that represents a "snapshot" of the original experience. Think of it as a film poster, albeit a moving one. The metaphoric image that captures the important theme or tension of the film, a theme or tension caused by links made in the past between roles, behaviors, and feelings that have been internalized by the traumatized person.

For Dora, what has been linked and internalized is a particular spin on the relationship between power and sex. But this time she will be the aggressor not the prey, the transgressor not the victim. By playing out the other side, she will have played both sides. She will have experienced this dynamic not only from the position of helplessness, but from the position of power. This takes courage because it forces on Dora a terrible truth she is finally able to tolerate—the knowledge of both vulnerability and cruelty that, under the right conditions, we are all capable of experiencing. With this knowledge, it is imaginable that she may ultimately be able to stop the wheel spinning, transcend this power dynamic, and move on.[15]

This is not to say that she and Peter will stop playing games. They may not want to. Only that the games will take on a different meaning. They will be about fun rather than about compulsion.[16]

DORA 1: *In bits and pieces my body slowly gave up its secrets. Memories flooded back.*

DORA II: *I remember my father's gas station. The pop machine is on the right. The long counter with the cash register is before me. There is a bubble-gum machine in the corner. Nothing else. The room is grimy, empty. No maps. No pyramids of oil cans. Nothing. I walk behind the counter and climb three steps into the back room. It is long and narrow. A dirty sink, dripping. An even dirtier toilet. There is no toilet seat, only the bare gummy porcelain. The smell of stale urine. In the corner is a cot, the mattress covered with an old army blanket. The walls of the room are papered with calendars of women. Girlie pictures. Pinups. A cheesecake. A dish. Chest thrust out, large breasts dangling. My favorite is a woman kneeling, half turned toward the camera, peeking over her shoulder. A pail and shovel on the sand beside her. Toys. The woman wears a bright red bathing suit. I reach out and lift the clear plastic that covers the picture. The plastic flies up and with it the patch of red that is the bathing suit. Underneath the woman is naked.*

My daddy raped me in that room. And the only ones who saw were the paper women gazing down from the wall.

To remember is to be able to tell the story. And this storytelling, this narration, is possibly all there is. As Roy Schafer writes in his book *Retelling a Life,* "Narrative is not an alternative to truth or reality; rather, it is the mode in which, inevitably, truth and reality are presented." So perhaps when a woman has been kept from the story of her incest, by either the safety of secrecy or the fragmentary nature of traumatic memory, the telling becomes essential. To tell the story is to make the moment real; to tell the story is to make her real.

There is a very suggestive video therapy used with some victims of trauma—primarily incest and combat—whose memories, encoded in a dissociative state, are inaccessible as narrative. People who cannot speak their story. This therapy is intriguing. Though it takes place in a clinical setting, this therapy replicates a similar, spontaneous process described by some women writers and artists.[17]

A woman is videotaped telling her story in an altered state; either hypnosis or sodium amytal is used.[18] It is only in this altered state that she can coherently tell her story. This video is then used as the central device in helping the patient construct and speak a narrative of her trauma in a state of normal consciousness. The woman first watches the video in subsequent sessions, which are also taped. These succeeding videos are of her watching herself watching and discussing the previous tape. These nested taped sessions go on until the woman is able to fill in the gaps and silences of her narrative and consciously tell a detailed and complete story of her trauma.

The tapes seem to create a distance from the traumatic moment, allowing her to reconstruct and tell the experience without drowning in feelings.[19] The critical element for mending seems to be the woman's ability to fill in the entire story without gaps and create a coherent narrative. The videotape is used, in the words of Louis Trinnin, to "reconstruct the fragmented traumatic memory so that it can become historical past rather than unfinished present." This echoes what Pierre Janet said about traumatic memory:

> A situation has not been satisfactorily liquidated . . . until we have achieved . . . an inward reaction through the words we address to ourselves, through the organization of the recital of the event to others and to ourselves, and through the putting of this recital in its place as one of the chapters in our personal history.[20]

With the creation of a narrative, a fragmented present tense becomes a coherent past tense. With distance comes detachment. A life is authored and reauthored. Narration is active. To narrate one's life is to have agency. To know and feel this agency is important for everyone, especially for those who have been victimized.

DORA I: *I hold my hands out in front of me, palms down. Peter looks at me. I meet his eyes with a level gaze and nod yes. Peter unbuckles his belt and draws it out.* "Make it real," *I tell him.*

"Are you sure?" *he asks.*

I'm absolutely sure. "Can't do it?"

"Oh, I can do it," *he says.*

Peter ties my hands together, picks me up and lays me on the bed. He lifts my hands over my head and ties them to the bed frame. Button by button he undoes my blouse. He places his open hand on my throat and slowly moves it down the front of my body—my chest, my breasts, my stomach. "Scared?" *he asks.*

"Yes," *I whisper.*

Peter jams his hand hard between my legs. "I'm in control now," *he says.* "Isn't that what you want?" *I nod my head, yes.* "What do you really want?" *asks Peter, his voice hard and cold.*

And I can't answer.

"I'm talking to you." *Peter sticks his face right up next to mine, his eyes malevolent.* "You want it rough?" *he says. The smell of stale urine. The pinups silently watching. I'm balled up on the cot, the cot, small as a mouse; my father approaches.*

"Fine," *he says,* "I'm going to stick it in your mouth. And there's nothing you can do about it."

Don't move, I think, maybe he won't see me.

"Dora," he whispers.

Thoughts freeze. Time perishes.

"Dora?"

I am no more.

Peter sits back and quickly unties my hands. His eyes soften with concern as he reaches out toward my face.

"Don't touch me!" I scream and leap off the bed. With a wide swing of my arm I sweep everything off my bureau—pictures, jewelry, books crash to the floor. I tug out the bureau drawers one by one and fling them across the room. Bras and T-shirts go flying. I lean against the bureau trying with all my might to heave it over. Peter grabs at me.

"Stop it," he yells. "You'll hurt yourself."

I turn on him and hiss, "Keep away!" Peter backs off.

I run to the closet and pull open the door. I grab skirts, blouses, sweaters and jerk them off their hangers. I blindly tear at the cloth, shredding it as ragged as my rage and grief. I pick up the chair and hurl it at the window. It smashes through the glass with a shattering explosion. I turn on Peter. "If I could I would blow up the fucking house."

DORA II: *In my mind's eye, the house blows up with such fiery force it's as if my brain itself will explode. Debris shoots to the sky, hangs in midair for the briefest of moments, then rains down to the earth. The fires will never burn out.*

DORA I AND II: *I reenter my body.*

DORA I: *Through the open window at my back, a soft breeze blows. The billowing curtain caresses my shoulder. I glance over to Peter, who sits across the room. I crawl over to him, picking my way through the mess I have made. I reach out my hand and tentatively touch his cheek. I feel his muscles tense beneath my fingertips. Looking into his eyes I know I have never felt such vulnerability before another human being. I risk a kiss. Tentative. Gentle. Peter hesitates for the briefest of moments, then returns my kiss with a tenderness and passion that I have never before experienced. I feel such love I think my heart will break. I surrender completely to the feeling; I know I am safe.*

DORA II: *That night I dream. I sit on the shore of a huge lake. The water is filled with women—my mother, Rosie, strangers—beckoning to me. It is hot in the sun. I want to swim but the water seems bottomless. Although I can look into it and see through its deep clearness, I know that dark things lurk at its bottom. I will drown if I enter. I look down into the water. The next moment I slip in.*

DORA I: *The water is warm and silky as I move beneath the surface.*

DORA II: *It is shallow here and when I look down I see it is tiled at the bottom with tiny squares of color.*

DORA I: *Red, purple, green, silver, gold. Intricate designs shining up through the clear water. I glide through the water with effortless strokes.*

DORA II: *The sun glistens off the surface. The tiles wink up at me. I know I can swim*

DORA I AND II: *forever.*

If the incest experience is transformative, then telling the story is yet another transformation. In constructing a narrative, fragments are knit into a whole; what has been shattered is cohered; a sense of self is restored. Narrative construction and integration of the self, regardless of which comes first, go hand in hand. This is an easy truth about narrative.

Here is a hard truth. Dora's pain lies, not only in the secret of the incest, but in the darker knowledge that the incest has brought her. In this sense, Dora loses her innocence twice. The first time as an eight-year-old child when, at the moment of rape, she peers into her father's soul and learns what a child should not have to know: the brutality of power, the ugliness of a corrupted desire, the cruelty of evil. Dora's second loss of innocence occurs when she finally remembers the incest. At that moment she understands the obliteration of her subjectivity that occurred when her father projected his own desires onto her. When he entered her body, she lost it to herself, spending her life living in reaction to the experience. She finally has the gift of her own subjectivity bought with the pain of this knowledge: she was not who she thought she was.

But there is another truth. The new narrative doesn't erase the old one. It stands beside it, a constant reminder of who we were, a never-ending, sometimes painful, contradiction. Both the Dora-of-the-Body and the Dora-of-the-Mind are authentic Doras. Past and present, unruly and controlling, victim and aggressor, both narratives are simultaneously true. Recognizing this requires that we expand our self-story to allow for contradiction and that we learn how to live with the unease it can cause us. Such knowledge forces a woman to be compassionate about herself, which, if she's lucky, can lead to an ability to move through the world with that same compassion, as well as depth, intelligence, judiciousness, and integrity. This is how I define the beginning of wisdom.

Pandora, though, is a fiction. Dora experiences herself differently in relationship to Peter, remembers her incest, and stops her self-cutting. She moves linearly from the inarticulate, if elegant, symptom, through the more dynamic enactment, to the direct telling of her incest story. Dora's drama, told from her singular point of view, comes from condensing and excluding. There are many other hidden stories here: Dora's relationship with her mother, both in the present and in the past; Dora's relationship with Joe; her friendship with Rosie; and her work with young children. And there are multiple authors of these stories, not only Dora, but also her mother, Peter, Joe, and even her father. And life has even more story lines yet. We change in fits and starts, and can rarely do it without the help of family, friends, therapists, enemies, and strangers. Our lives are authored and reauthored, but they are also coauthored.

There is no way to adequately end Dora's story. As Tim O'Brien has said about all war stories, if it has a moral or an ending, you know it's not real. So let me end with another story instead, this time one of my own.

We don't always choose our topics; sometimes they choose us. And often, because it's unconscious, it can take years to figure this out.

It is not without meaning, I think, that I became a filmmaker. In 1972 I was halfway through a doctorate in cognitive psychology, a field that studies the brain and mind, a field as distant from the body as possible. Then I stumbled into a film course. I sat in a darkened classroom for five hours every Friday afternoon and watched images. Not narratives, but avant-garde films by Maya Deren, Bruce Baillie, Jordan Belson, Carolee Schneeman, Stan Brakhage, and others. I had never known images could speak so eloquently about feelings and experiences: family, birth, sexuality, everyday moments. Here was a language rich in subtlety, complexity, and meaning. I vividly remember the moment I knew that I would leave psychology and become a filmmaker. I wrote in my journal: "Film will give me the voice I have always craved. Images will allow me to speak." And so I became a filmmaker.

From 1973 on I made films about issues of historical importance to women, including, of course, myself. *Self Defense* (1973) metaphorically represented the emotional exhilaration of the early years of the second-wave women's movement. *Parthenogenesis* (1975) was about the conflicts of being a woman making art. *Daughter Rite* (1978) explored the emotional landscape of mothers and daughters. *What You Take For Granted . . .* (1983) examined the contradictions of women working in fields traditionally dominated by men.

I defined these films as political, and still think they are. They present public models of what women strive for, with all the inherent contradictions (becoming a concert violinist like Rosie in *Parthenogenesis*); show us our selves, larger than life, up there on the screen (the carpenter, sculptor, educator, doctor, truck driver, and cable splicer in *What You Take For Granted* . . .); and give us permission for feelings we do not dare speak (*Daughter Rite*). My films were intended to validate the women in the audience in all their lived contradictions. My experience showing these films has borne this out. But these films also validated me. Not by giving voice to my "self," but rather by giving me a way to construct my "self."

On the most obvious level, the films gave me a way to negotiate through my world. I had a problem—my confusion and isolation as a woman artist in the early seventies, my complex emotional relationship with my mother, or my contradictory position in the workplace—and so I made a movie. Making these films, especially *Daughter Rite* and *What You Take For Granted* . . . gave me the illusion that I was in control of those things over which I had no control at all. For instance, it is interesting to me that *What You Take For Granted* . . . , a film in which women boldly talk about succeeding against the odds in a male-defined and dominated work world, was made just before I came up for tenure at Northwestern University, the first woman in my field there to do so.

But these films also served a more subtle function of self-definition. By making them, I was someone who could harness resources—money, equipment, people—meaning that I possessed sophisticated management, producing, and interpersonal skills. I could carry a complex project through to completion, which meant I was probably responsible and certainly not a quitter. And my films, with their breaking of categories, meant that being different was more important to me than imitation. My self-definition, as mirrored by my work, read like a recommendation I wrote for myself: Michelle is a self-starter, good with people, takes creative risks.

Most important, however, was that the very existence of these films was evidence that I was someone who had both a voice and something to say. My films gave me a presence in the world. Through them I became authorized, that is, they gave me the authority to become the author of my life, the protagonist in my own narrative. But what did this protagonist want to say? And why did the form through which I spoke evolve from experimental to more conventional narrative film language?

I started out as an avant-garde filmmaker, making short, abstract, "structuralist" films, an experiment with pure movement connected to the formal exploration of much twentieth-century art. While I was deeply committed to formal play, I conceptualized each film as a visual metaphor to express a concrete moment of lived experience. *Self Defense* was an exploration of filmic movement *and* the empowerment of the women's movement. *April 3, 1973* was really about the compression of time *and* the anxiety of being a woman trying to pack everything in: a relationship, a career, a politically committed life. The formal experimentation of these films was readily understood by my audience while, at the same time, their abstraction obscured the underlying lived experience.[21]

Adrienne Rich, in her book *On Lies, Secrets, and Silence,* writes about her own early poetry: "Formalism . . . [was] like asbestos gloves, it allowed me to handle materials I couldn't pick up barehanded." This is how formalism functioned for me. It taught me the pleasure of images and something of how images communicate, in both the aesthetic and affective realms. It also kept me safe; by expressing feelings and fleeting moments, it contained that which I wasn't prepared to touch.

There is a suggestive resemblance between my own artistic evolution from an experimental to a more traditional narrative film form and what much neurobiological, cognitive, and clinical psychological research tells us about memory, both traumatic and explicit. The formalism of my experimental films, with their fragmentation, strong imagery, and affective associations split off from narrative, closely parallels the current understanding of traumatic memory as an experience in which knowledge, emotions, and narrative are severed from one another.

My early abstract films were always about fragmentation or the movement from fragmentation to wholeness. For instance, *Integration* (1974) takes twenty-five still images of the solitary woman violinist in her bedroom and rephotographs them to give unity, temporality, and movement to that which was fragmented, discontinuous, and still. Clearly I was trying to do something here.

The formalism of my films protected me well. Once I moved away from a purely experimental manipulation of images and started putting actors—integrated, talking, acting bodies—into my films, there was this driving unconscious need to always include at least one scene in which a woman told a traumatic body story.

In both *Daughter Rite* and *What You Take For Granted* . . . there is a moment at which a woman character tells a story about sexual abuse. When I wrote and filmed these scenes, I had not yet consciously come to terms with my own experience of incest. What's even more extraordinary is that the stories told by Stephanie in *Daughter Rite* and Dianna in *What You Take For Granted* . . . are structurally similar. They are both tales of sexual abuse committed by a man on a girl child's body. In both instances, the abuse is unstoppable and the girl child is inconsolable because of an ineffectual woman.

In *Daughter Rite* the stepfather, Henry, rapes Stephanie and says to her as he leaves her room, "If you know what's good for you, you're not going to tell your mother about this." Stephanie tries to tell her mother, but her mother betrays her by being unable to hear what she has to say: "[She] cut me off right there, she just cut me off. She turned around and looked in the mirror and started fixing her hair and telling me what she'd had for dinner . . ." In *What You Take For Granted* . . . an eight-year-old girl is raped by her older brother's friend. "We played love," she says. Dianna, the doctor who tells the story, is powerless to help. When she angrily confronts the other doctors for mocking the eight-year-old rape victim brought into the emergency room, she's reported to the hospital director. Dianna recounts the doctor telling her "I had acted very immaturely . . . I had to learn how to handle my emotions if I was going to be a doctor. He said to me, 'You're a doctor, act like one.'"

These stories are told by "talking heads," characters who look directly into the camera and speak. Since they occur in films that also include more actively embodied scenes, i.e., scenes that are acted and acted out, this is a meaningful aesthetic choice. The use of a "talking head" to describe terrifying moments of child rape protected me from risking that which I was not yet ready to risk. This became my aesthetic strategy of displacement, simultaneously revealing and obscuring my secret. The "talking heads" allowed me to speak incest without feeling incest. They allowed me to talk about incest without really talking about *my* incest. By using an actor to speak the stories of the women I had interviewed, I was doubly protected from my own experience, doubly displaced.

The formal experimentation of my films, with their images plucked from narrative, kept me safe until a different kind of formal structure—narrative itself, with its linear unfolding, dramatic tension, characters who act, and action imbued with affect—enabled me to finally speak.

In 1989, a year after my mother spoke the terrible secret of her own sexual abuse, I became severely ill with acute, uncontrolled asthma, and with the asthma came insomnia. At first the lack of breath would awaken me. This was followed in time by terrifying flashbacks: images and body sensations unbound from story.

Desperate to distract myself, I turned to the familiar and safe—my work. Much to my surprise, I began writing a narrative, Dora's story and that of her mother, Emma, which follows in the next chapter. *Pandora* was difficult to write. Having spent nearly fifteen years developing a language of images and fragmentation, I lacked even an intuitive grasp of the basics of conventional storytelling. I sat at my desk night after night, overwhelmed by the idea of narrative. Yet I struggled to write out of a deep, unnamed need, and I slowly learned.

One day I was confronted with the reality that *Pandora* had no ending, no emotional catharsis, no epiphany, and I hadn't the first clue how to find or create one. I sat and stared hopelessly at the computer screen for hours. Then unexpectedly, as is often the case, the muse dropped in and offered the pivotal scene I needed. My fingers punched the keys; the words flashed onto the monitor's screen with a warm amber glow. I reread my scene. It was perfect. The narrative was complete. I turned off the computer with a feeling of accomplishment and an odd sense of relief.

That night I awakened at three o'clock, trembling and gasping for breath. Possessed by a deep apprehension, I turned on my computer and revisited the day's work. The scene I read on the screen was not as I remembered. It was not about Dora at all. It was about me. There in bright, pulsating words was *my* name and *my* story of the ongoing sexual abuse I had experienced as a child with my grandfather.

The terror I felt in that moment came from the shock of being so fully cut off from an essential part of myself. My body and unconscious knew what my intellect had not remembered. If I couldn't depend on my intellect, the thing I trusted most, then I was lost. My primary way of being in the world was shattered. Yet, at the same time, I experienced profound release. I was in awe of my unconscious, which had led me to this place in my work. It was a moment of despair and abandonment, wonderment and hope.

I inched toward a narrative fully informed by the emotional in my work as my own incest story reached closure. My flashbacks of incest cohered into an intelligible narrative as my films and writing became more storylike. The two processes mutually supported each another. The verbal access to my own incest narrative enabled me to write Dora's story while, simultaneously, Dora's narrative carried me further into my own story of childhood incest with my bad grandfather, who, unlike Abraham, my good grandfather, did not innocently lay down beside me.

Pandora became the fiction that told a truth. Yet much still remains lost; gaps and fissures endure. These losses do not belie the fact of my incest, an experience that has been corroborated by members of my family. Rather, absences and confusions are the hallmark of all remembrances. Memory is an incomplete and fragile process.

I remember vividly the night I received the phone call from my mother telling me that my grandfather had died. I was living in Madison, Wisconsin, finishing my last year of graduate school, and I had to fly back to

Boston for his funeral. I remember packing my suitcase. I remember the ride to the airport. I remember boarding the DC-10 for the flight home and the red, gold, and blue of my seat's upholstery. I remember nothing else: not landing, not my father waiting for me at the airport, not the funeral. When my grandfather was entombed in the earth, I was set free. Yet I'm robbed of my moment of release. Every time I try to retrieve the memory, to place myself in a history I know I inhabited, I slam into an impenetrable wall. I cannot break or claw or see through to the memory that dwells on the other side.

I sometimes ask my sister, or my mother, to tell me the story of my grandfather's funeral: who was there, what was said, what I wore. I keep hoping their stories will trigger my own. As Carolyn Steedman has written in her book *Past Tenses*, "The telling of a life story is a *confirmation* of that self that stands there telling the story." I yearn for narrative; without it I am silenced. So as I wait to more fully find my own story, I write the story of others.

In representing the incest trauma, experimental and narrative film strategies can have very different meanings and functions for the author than they do for the viewer. For the filmmaker, narrative can integrate experiences for which memory has not always functioned adequately. Narrative renders the incomprehensible understandable. Narrative offers the much needed illusions of coherency and cause and effect where there were none. Narrative puts the author at ease. For the audience, however, narrative reduces a complex, confusing, overdetermined tidal wave of experiences and half-found awareness into something that is linear, understandable. It cleans up the trauma, makes it tidy, and makes it, at the structural level, familiar. Narrative makes it seem safe. This is a lie. Everything that makes narrative honest for the author is precisely what makes it false for the audience. Pieces not wholeness, discontinuity not fluidity, is a more authentic language for the expression of trauma and its aftermath.

The paradox is this: To make the incest experience comprehensible, we must speak in narrative. For the listener, this does violence to the experience, which is more authentically expressed through the fragmented images and sounds of an experimental film practice. Yet that very same story, simultaneously, helps the woman (or man) who has experienced such trauma to transform the experience and with it her sense of herself and the world.

The relationship between psyche and art is mysterious and humbling. My art storehoused fragments of my story until I was able to verbalize it, becoming, eventually, the vehicle through which I had the longed-for conversation with myself. In this way art inhabits the axis between the conscious and the unconscious. It is both the message and the messenger. In this pivotal position it sounds a cautionary note: to be alert to aesthetic choices and the weight and meaning that formal devices carry. Remembering all the time the great power of those things we cannot and do not consciously know.

The Simple Act of Seeing

*I don't know anything in the world more mysterious than desire
in its manifestations, its appearances, its disappearances.*
::   Monique Wittig and Sande Zeig, *Lesbian Peoples:
       Material for a Dictionary* (1976)

GRANDMOTHER: Every night I wake at the bottom of a deep black pit. Way
above me floats a small saucer of light getting smaller and smaller as it
closes up over my head. Every night I wake and feel my life closing in.
Every. Single. Night. I'm terror-crazed of dying. My best friend, Beckka,
when she was a girl, she died. Or they thought she died. She caught the in-
fluenza, you know. She was already laid out at the funeral home, the undertaker about to drain her body. He was leaning over her, his embalming
stick above her chest when—she opened her eyes.

GRANDDAUGHTER: This is a story about mothers and daughters—real ones,
imaginary ones, and the relationship between the two. I've told this story
before, with *Daughter Rite,* when I was thirty years old. Now at forty-
eight, I'm once again telling the tale. My mother inspired the fiction of
Daughter Rite; nineteen years later it is my grandmother who plays the
muse. Different textures, different inflections, a different time, yet the same
song singing round and round in my head.

It is not surprising that I tried first to understand my mother and had
to wait for midlife to take on my grandmother. My mother was easy, or so
I thought, for it was onto her that I projected all that I refused to see in myself: female weakness, vulnerability, and victimization. My grandmother, on
the other hand, was more formidable: passionate, demanding, and fierce.

The immediate world of my childhood was bound by my mother
and anchored by my grandmother, who stood at the center of both my
mother's world and my own. It is my mother and grandmother I need to

understand. It is myself as a daughter, essentially shaped by a mother and her mother, that I strive to know. Although I do, of course, recognize that I can never really know. "It is hard to write about my mother," declares Adrienne Rich in *Of Woman Born*, "Whatever I do write, it is my story I am telling, my version of the past. If she were to tell her own story other landscapes would be revealed."

The character of my story is named Emma, which was not my grandmother's name, in order to emphasize distance between the real woman—Anne—and my imaginary one. Emma floats in the narrow current between fact and fiction, between the verifiably certain and the embellishments of wishful fantasy. Emma's story has fidelity to many of the details of my grandmother Anne's life and is a work of my imagination. This doesn't make Emma's story untrue. Quite the contrary. Fiction reframes the world, and in the shift leads us into the hidden rooms of our interior lives, where inchoate truths linger. Fiction reveals truths—more sensed than known—that lie at the crossroads of self-story and biography. Fiction allows me to have a dialogue with myself when writing about my mother and grandmother. Out of this struggle is created a narrative that reveals something about the mother-daughter experience as it unfolds across three generations of women in a working-class Jewish family in mid–twentieth century America.

GRANDMOTHER: One night my husband, Jack, he finally blew. "Whore!" he screamed, his breath hitting my face.

I stood for a heartbeat, tasting the stale cigar smoke that hung in the air, holding my rage. Then I looked him straight in the eye and said, "Don't ever, *ever* talk to me like that again." And I meant it. And he knew it. He turned his back on me and stomped out of that room. "Don't you dare walk out on me," I said, real coldlike, "I'm talking to you." But he just kept on walking. "To hell with you!" I screamed.

And then I heard him, somewhere off in the distance, throw at Dory, "You'll grow up to be just like her . . . Ehhhh!" The gall of the man.

"Dora!" I yelled, and Dory, my granddaughter, eight years old, my special one, comes through the archway and shuffles toward me. I scoop her up and squeeze her to me tight.

GRANDDAUGHTER: There is much I don't know about my grandmother's childhood, just a few facts shifted down from my mother about her own mother. Although my grandmother's name was Anne, we called her Nana, and she was the youngest of thirteen children. Her father, Solomon, was Dutch and grew up in the Jewish ghetto of Amsterdam, where he hand-rolled cigars. Her mother, Leah, was born in England and spoke with the broad cockney accent of the lower classes; Leah's own mother was Portuguese, her father Spanish. This meant my grandmother was descended from Sephardic Jews who, expelled from Spain during the 1492 Inquisition, wandered north, in and out of whatever country would have them over the next four hundred years.

Leah aspired to migrate to America, the land of opportunity, but Sol resisted. Leah prevailed and the family, then with twelve children, packed up and shipped out to the new world, only to have Sol's anxiety and homesickness drag them back to the old. Four times they made the round-trip journey, sometimes returning to Amsterdam, other times to London. Leah, not one to give up, pleaded, wheedled, or perhaps blackmailed; there were the children to think about after all. Sol, no match for his wife, gave in or gave up and the family crossed over the Atlantic one fifth and final time to settle in Boston. My grandmother was born soon after they arrived, their only child to be birthed on American soil. Leah was fifty-two years old; Anne was her change-of-life baby. The year was 1897.

GRANDMOTHER: Every night when my daughter May came in from work, we'd sit together on the couch and talk and she'd catch me up on her day. Usually what her jerk-of-a-boss did, like how he wouldn't give her a break even though it's that time of the month and her cramps were so bad she almost threw up. "He hates me," she'd say.

"No," I'd tell her, "he's just an SOB. Like most of them." We'd sit together on that couch and talk, so close that as we breathed our bodies touched.

Dory would be cross-legged on the floor not saying peep, her nose, as usual, buried in a book. But nothing went by her, not a damn thing.

One night May says "Here" and hands me a package bundled up in brown paper, tied with a big yellow bow. She's smiling, so proud of herself as I tear it open and tug at a corner of satiny fabric. I keep pulling and it keeps coming until a huge, gold bedsheet floats onto my lap. Real, honest-to-God silk. I rub it soft to my face. "Oh, honey, it's . . . luxurious. You make me feel like a queen!"

My daughter beams and tells me, "I saw it and knew it was you."

I want to see how I look wrapped in my high-class sheet so I tell her to get me a mirror.

My daughter turns to Dory, "Get your grandmother a mirror." Dory has her head still stuck in that book and pretends not to hear. "I'm talkin' to you, young lady," May says.

"Let her be," I tell her, "You go get the mirror." My daughter balks for a heartbeat, then pushes herself off the couch and goes fetching. Dory has not moved, not even to turn the page.

Jack comes up behind me and rests his hand on my shoulder, playing with the silky sheets. He slides his hand down across my breast and plays there, too. I slap it away. "Not in front of the children," I tell him.

GRANDDAUGHTER: I spent the first nineteen years of my life as the youngest of three generations of women—grandmother, daughter, and granddaughters—living together under one roof. I experienced myself as a daughter to two different mothers, also a mother and daughter, who lived together for fifty-six years.

We women maneuvered around each other and endlessly aligned and realigned. My mother was simultaneously a mother to me and a daughter to her own mother, one moment carrying an adult's authority, the next a child herself, still clinging to her own mother's skirts, unable to hold her own. At the same time, Nana had a sense of proportion toward me that she often lacked with her own daughter, who equally lacked that sense toward her daughter. When my mother, fearing for my safety on the harsh city streets, refused to buy me a bicycle, Nana surprised me with a second-hand model outfitted with balloon tires and a new coat of pink paint on its round, bulbous frame. Later, during my tumultuous teenage years when my mother would demand, "Where do you think you're going in that outfit? Only prostitutes wear fishnets," Nana, winking at me behind her daughter's back, would soothe, "Now, honey, they're just the fashion. Things are different than when we were girls."

Nana inevitably teased my mother into letting me have my way while simultaneously ordering her own daughter to hem her dress, pick a few things up at the market, and drive her to play poker, tasks my mother willingly, lovingly performed. Enjoying the dependence of her own daughter, Nana encouraged independence in me, the chosen heir to the throne of her matriarchy. And I, taking advantage of the shifting sands, learned to smoothly play my mother and grandmother against each other.

Many daughters split their one mother into different, often contradictory, roles against which they test and measure their evolving selfhood: other-directed versus inner-directed, self-sacrificing versus self-actualizing, conformist versus daring. Or, if lucky, they find two separate mothers to embody the polarities. Adrienne Rich, in *Of Woman Born*, describes these two mothers as "the biological [mother] who represents the culture of domesticity, of male-centeredness, of conventional expectations, and another, perhaps a woman artist or teacher, who becomes the countervailing figure." Sophie Freud, in her book *My Three Mothers and Other Passions*, talks of the many mothers throughout her life, but focuses specifically on two: the biological "bad mother" of her childhood, whom she found distant and bitter, and the "good mother" of her late midlife, her aunt Anna Freud, from whom she learned to love.

Nana was born just before the century turned and she mothered her son and daughter during the jazzy twenties. After her first two children, three more pregnancies were terminated with crude and painful life-threatening abortions. Years later she matter-of-factly told me that she loved her son and daughter and simply couldn't afford another mouth to feed.

My mother was born in 1920 and she mothered me and my sister during a different time, the fifties, when women flooded from the workplace back into the home; she embraced her homemaker role, subsuming her own needs in devotion to husband and children. My mother had worked as a secretary, a bookkeeper, a public relations release writer, a saleswoman, a proofreader, and an assembler of baby slippers until her marriage in her late twenties and she deeply desired to live out the postwar myth, trudging back into the workplace only on occasion when forced by my father's low pay to bring home much-needed money. To me, Nana's rebelliousness shined against my mother's conformity, my grandmother's daylong poker games with her women friends seeming much more romantic than the banality of my mother's *Family Circle* recipes stuffed into the kitchen drawers, yellowing with age. Later when I discovered feminism, my grandmother seemed downright heroic, my mother a timorous dupe of the patriarchy. My images of both these women, reductionist and unjust, served me well.

GRANDMOTHER: Nate—he's my boss at the factory—often dropped by for dinner and he always brought a treat, usually steaks. Always the gentleman.

So the four of us are sitting around the table sorting our hands and Nate starts talking about a trip he and his wife are planning down to Miami. And his bird-of-a-wife chirps up, "I've always wanted to stay at the Fontainebleau, right there on the beach, you know. Nate's such a lambie-pie. I'm out," she says and she throws in her cards.

Jack glances down at his hand, then looks right at Nate. "Call me pat," he says. "I'll stand on it."

Just then Dory comes shuffling in, a book dangling from her hand, and she gives me a goodnight kiss.

And Nate, of course, says in that big way of his, "Come on down with us, we'll have a great time."

Jack tosses a quarter onto the table and casually says to no one in particular, "We can't."

I tell Dory to get me a glass of water. She doesn't need to hear all this.

Then Nate deals himself one more card. "Why not? We'll fly over to Havana for a night or two."

And Jack looks right at me and says, "No, we're ah . . . a little short of cash this month." And he tosses another quarter into the center of the table and chases it with a dollar bill.

I keep my mouth shut and match his bet.

Nate smiles, "So what? Don't let that stop you. My treat. Business is booming." And then he turns to me, "What do you say?"

Dory sets the glass of water down by my hand with a hard splash. I can tell she doesn't miss a trick.

"Hey, did ya forget my kiss?" says Jack, then he tosses in another dollar, this time followed by a five.

I watch as Dory leans in and kisses the air beside her grandfather's face. Jack, distracted by the stakes, doesn't notice that her kiss doesn't connect. I look at the five-dollar bill lying like a dead fish on the table, then I look over to Jack. "You fool," I tell him and fold my cards down, "I'm out." Now it's just Jack and Nate in the game.

Nate lays a stack of dollars down and neatly fans them out. I count ten. "I call," he says, smiling.

Jack lays down his hand—he holds three nines.

Nate slowly turns over his cards—a full house: three sevens and a pair of deuces.

He rakes in the bills and change. Then he reaches out and snags Dory by the waist. "Got a kiss for your Uncle Nate?" he asks. Dory stiffens but allows the kiss. Nate pulls a quarter out of her ear. "What's this? It must be yours," he teases. Dory twists out of his grasp, ignoring the money.

"Say thank you," I tell her.

Dory takes the quarter. Reluctantly. "Thank you," she mumbles under her breath.

"You know better than that."

"So what do you say?" he asks me again. "Let's all go down to the sunny south and play."

"Maybe we'd better not," I tell him. "You give us too much already."

Nate smiles. "What are friends for?"

GRANDDAUGHTER: The most wounding fight my mother and I ever had was over money. I was sixteen years old and had been working for two years in the statistical department of a large Boston insurance company. Three days a week after school, all day Saturday, and every vacation I sat five rows back, three columns over, in a cavernous, fluorescent-lit room of one hundred desks, updating by hand the weekly payments made to insured workers on disability. It was numbing work, now done by computers, insulting work, where we were required to raise our hands for permission to go to the bathroom—one at a time—and were publicly scolded if we spoke to our neighbor. One hundred women in an air hangar of a room; the men in their private offices that circled around us on the periphery of the floor.

A room full of women. Women who carried their lunches to work, foil-wrapped homemade Italian meatball sandwiches dripping with juice and marinara, made by their mothers in East End basement kitchens. Women whose most prized possessions were their sapphire engagement rings, diamonds being only a rich woman's fancy. Women who closed their account books, covered their adding machines, and surreptitiously slicked on their lipstick hunched over their desks as the minute hand clicked its last three stops on its way to the quitting bell at 4:55. All these women— girls just out of high school, working mothers, older single women—were biding their time until rescued by either husbands or death. I was the only girl, literally one in one hundred, whose escape would be college.

Every Friday I handed my paycheck over to my mother, who would use much of it for the week's food and rent, banking the leftovers in my college savings account. Then one day I discovered, to my horror, that our shiny, new pink refrigerator had been bought with this college savings. My mother had cleaned out the account. In one instant of indulgent consumption, she had cheated me out of both my education and my deliverance from the family. Blinded from rationality or understanding by my now bleak future, I hurled bile: Mean. Greedy. Spendthrift. I told her she would never see another paycheck. She told me I was selfish. I said that I needed all my money for college since she obviously wasn't going to provide. She said that I was part of the family and had to contribute my share like everyone else and anyway, there was always the state teachers college, virtually free. I screamed, a teacher! Over my dead body. She screamed, contribute, young lady, or you can just take care of yourself. Not one red cent from me! I screamed, fine, and stomped out of her bedroom.

In this feverish moment my mother clinched her title as Bad Mother. And around my panic formed a wale of bitterness that festered over the years as I worked my way through college and life. My mother nursed her own lacerations. Like mother, like daughter, like mother.

Daughter Rite is a story told exclusively from the daughter's point of view. It is only the daughters who speak; everything we learn about the mother is filtered through their voices. At the time I made the film, I was incapable of imagining the mother's story; I was still too angry at mine.

The Narrator-daughter in *Daughter Rite* self-righteously believes she understands her mother better than the mother understands herself. Harsh toward what she perceives as her mother's dishonesty and self-deception, she describes her mother as "foolish and impractical." When the mother can't make her mortgage payments and loses her house, the daughter proclaims it was "a ridiculous fantasy in the first place." Throughout the film the daughter characterizes her mother with a sharp tongue, calling her bitter, intrusive, manipulative, dishonest, controlling, and unsexual, this last the most revealing.

The film's supreme moment of tenderness occurs when the mother gives her daughter a gift of silk pajamas, the last remnant of her trousseau saved all those years in the bottom of a drawer. The pajamas overtly express the mother's romantic dreams, which, having been preserved in tissue paper, she offers to her daughter. But these are trousseau pajamas, vibrating with the hum of marriage, wedding night, and sex. If the mother ever had a vibrant sexual life, she doesn't anymore; it's been packed away for a long time. Here is a clue to where the daughter's real anger lies: entangled in sex.

The film's pivotal scene unfolds as Stephanie, the youngest daughter, looks directly into the lens of the camera and tells of the rape by her stepfather and her mother's subsequent inability to acknowledge it. Describing the rape itself Stephanie is cool and detached. It is only when she tells of her mother's denial of the rape that tears and anger flow. The daughter's betrayal by her mother is deeply, furiously felt. The film offers no exploration of why the mother behaves as she does; this is the daughter's film, after all. By making *Daughter Rite*, I, the daughter, in turn betray the mother by refusing to understand her actions. I get my revenge; I blame her.

In writing Emma's story I finally reach for the mother's point of view. Emma is a woman not exclusively defined by her motherhood, a mother with her own desires and needs of psyche, heart, and body. My grandmother had a twenty-year love affair while married to my grandfather. This fact is all that either my mother or I really know. Emma's story is my truth of that fact. My mother tells a different truth. Our dissimilar versions reveal more about each of us than about the woman we are both trying to understand. By my mother's account, her mother was trapped into the affair by her husband and kept there by him for the money and goods it brought into the household. Her mother was acted upon. In my imagination Nana was the protagonist who set everything in motion.

GRANDMOTHER: It was Sunday morning and Jack was at the garage working his shift. May was still asleep. Dory was probably in bed reading. And I was in my bedroom . . . watching the top of my lover's bald head sway back and forth as he nuzzled my breast. Nate pinched my nipple and reeled me right back into my body. I giggled and slapped his hand away. He pinched me again. I giggled and gave him another playful slap. He buried his face in my neck and nuzzled some more.

And then, God knows why, I looked up.

Dory stood in the doorway staring right through me.

I gazed at her over my lover's head. What could I say?

And then she vanished.

Nate's still nuzzling, oblivious to the world. I push him away, "You've gotta go now," I tell him. I could tell he didn't want to. "Go. Go," I say.

He got up, pulled on his pants, found some bills in his wallet, and held them out to me. "Why don't you buy yourself a little something?" he said.

I flash my smile and hate myself as my fingers fold around money.

GRANDDAUGHTER: When I was in graduate school, the man I lived with through much of my twenties came home to meet my family. At the end of the weekend, he asked why I had never admitted that I was working class. The label fit, smoothly explaining the feelings of outsidedness I had experienced throughout my childhood and adolescence.

When I was eleven we moved to a more upscale suburb. Yet rather than experiencing upward mobility, I felt only social confusion. My neighborhood playmates were the children of hardworking, blue-collar fathers; being Catholic, they all went to parochial school. My schoolmates, on the other hand, were the children of Jewish professionals who lived in the new ranch houses in another part of town. Their homes, filled with books and encyclopedias, Danish modern furniture and soft pastel colors, were in stark contrast to my family's rococo dwelling of gold and red flocked wallpaper, heavy carved furniture, and chromed bathroom faucets antiqued "gold," turning green over time. This home was mirrored more by the loud chaos of *Life of Riley* and *The Honeymooners* than by *Father Knows Best* and *Leave It to Beaver*, where genteel families sat down for genteel dinners at which dads quietly inquired about what happened in school.

Did the working-class label fit so well because my grandfather pumped gas? Because my father, despite working in his own father's ragman business as a salesman, couldn't make enough money? Because in the multigenerational home of my childhood it was my working-class grandfather, not my peddler-class father, who set the tone? Because I was the first generation in my family to get a college education? Because in the academic world in which I moved, working class succinctly defined my lack of shared experiences with my middle-class colleagues? Or was it just easier to feel the otherness of class rather than the otherness of sexual abuse? And perhaps the simplest way to describe a childhood dominated by women?

Carolyn Steedman, in writing about her own working-class childhood, describes how, for children of working-class families, it is often the mother and not the father who embodies power. The child experiences a father who is relatively powerless in the larger social world outside the home, so that even if he is physically predatory, as my grandfather was, he can simultaneously be perceived as a weak man. The men in my family, my grandfather and father, were dominated by Nana, who used her emotional and sexual authority to control the home. This undercut the influence of my two fathers and I "possessed a generalized apprehension that it is women who dictate the immediate terms of life."

I have always taken the power of women more seriously than the power of men. My father was a good man and parent who was not of this world of women and thus my emotional life didn't revolve around him. It was the mothers of my family who could give and take, it was the mothers who could betray. That is why it is the betrayal of my grandmother, and not that of my grandfather, that so deeply cuts.

Nana did not offer unconditional love. She demanded fidelity from her family: son, daughter, spouses, and four grandchildren. Sundays we would gather together. When we, the grandchildren, were young, we'd dress up for a big afternoon dinner out at a fancy Boston restaurant. Later, when we grew older, we'd gather at the house reading the Sunday paper, playing gin rummy, kibitzing the day away. My aunt, who resented my grandmother, refused to come for these Sunday visits and eventually my uncle, caught between his wife and his mother, refused to come, too. Nana, furious at her son's split loyalty, threatened to slice him out of her life if he didn't resume his Sunday visits. My uncle, for perhaps the first and only time, stood up to his mother. And she did cut him off, cleanly and forever, refusing, until the day she died years later, to see him again. The lesson was not lost on me.

GRANDMOTHER: Jack was in the kitchen fiddling with his watch while Dory set the table for dinner. I stood at the stove frying up thin strips of meat—dipping them in batter, coating them with flour, placing them in the hot oil of the electric fry pan. The sounds of a happy home—sizzling oil, scraping flint, clinking dishes.

Jack told Dory to run down to the basement and get him the small needle-nose pliers.

"Finish setting the table," I told her.

"I asked her to do something for me."

"Not now," I told him. "Dinner's ready."

So Jack turned to me and said real slylike, "Nate hasn't been around lately."

Dory set the plate down with a loud clatter and I shot her a look. She squirmed. "Sorry."

I told him things were busy at the factory, so he suggested in that butter-would-melt-in-his-mouth voice of his that I give Nate a call. "And just when do I have time?" I said. "Dory, the forks go on the left of the plate. You know that."

"Call him after dinner," says Jack.

"Nate's not coming over," I say and tell Dory, "Go down and get the pliers."

Dory whines, "I'm not done setting the table."

"I said now!" Dory backs out of the room.

Jack goes to the sink and washes his hands. "So why don't you wash up at the station?" I say. "You stink of gas."

"Sink's broken. So, why?"

"Why what?"

"Why isn't Nate coming over?"

I turn and look him in the eye, "God, you've got chutzpah. Because I told him not to, that's why." Jack just grunts.

"It's over."

"Oh. Really."

"Enough already!" I dump the fried meat out of the pan into a heap on his plate.

Jack pushes it away. "This is dreck."

"It's all there is."

"I want steak," says Jack and he gets up from the table and stomps out of the room.

"Bring home more money then!" I scream at his disappearing back. I fling the plate, meat and all, at the doorway. It hits the wall and slides down, leaving a slimy trail on the yellow tile.

GRANDDAUGHTER: My mother dominated my father in subtle, but significant ways. The family checking account was in her name and every Friday night my father would come home and hand over his pay, folded into a small brown envelope. On the outside, scratched in pencil, were columns of tiny neat figures—M 2.05, T 1.95, W 2.00, R 2.00, F 1.95—accounting for the money he had spent on lunch for the week. My mother returned a small allowance to my father for his next week's meals, parceling the rest out to the various creditors, always waiting. My mother came by this power directly and honestly, from the example set by her mother.

My mother's childhood was bound by the economic growth of the twenties, which did not touch her, and the depression, which deeply did. Her parents moved often in her childhood, from Boston, where her father sold vegetables off a cart, to Chicago, where he briefly found work in a shoe factory. They then moved back to Massachusetts, where he held down a series of jobs: shoe cutter, corner store shopkeeper, milkman, gas station jockey, and finally shipping room clerk. My grandfather was a man who, though he worked hard, continually got laid off, and even when working, never brought home enough money. Nana's work—standing on a line in a candy factory, selling dresses in a small shop—was absolutely essential. When she finally found an easier source of income—the wealthy family friend who was her lover for twenty years—her power over her husband cohered.

GRANDMOTHER: Jack grabbed my arm and dragged me away from the bureau and then he pulled open the drawer. I slammed it shut and threw myself against it, blocking him. A bottle of perfume, my most expensive one, smashed to the floor and Jack took that moment to push me away and open the drawer. I wasn't quick enough and he grabbed the handful of money. It's mine, not his. I tried to pry the bills from his fingers. He just slipped my grasp. I was caught off balance and fell on the bed. He looked down at me in contempt. "You're just a whore," he said, and left.

I started to cry at the unfairness of it all. I heard a rustle and looked up, expecting to see Jack standing there, ready to apologize. It was Dory. She reached out and petted me like she would a dog.

"Don't cry," she said. "Please don't cry. I'll get Mommy."

"No!" I screamed, "*No!* Get me a hankie."

Dory fetched a hankie from the bureau and climbed onto the bed. I blew my nose. I buttoned my bathrobe, plumped up the pillows, and crawled under the covers.

"Why's Poppa mad at you?" asked Dory.

"He's not mad."

"He yelled at you."

"That's the way married people talk to each other," I told her, knowing it was a lie.

"Is he mad about Uncle Nate?"

I asked her why she said that. "He kisses you," she said.

"He kisses you too and Poppa doesn't get mad at you, does he?"

And then she said, "Are you a 'hore like Poppa says you are?"

I smacked her across the face. Oh, God.

Instinctively I reached out to her and she cringed. I was horrified.

I pulled back the covers and motioned for Dory to crawl in beside me. "Come here," I pleaded. She wouldn't budge. "I love you, honey. You know you're my special one. Come on. I'm sorry." And still Dory wouldn't move. Tears sprung hot in my eyes and I decided that if she'd do this one thing, come to me, it'd be a sign I wasn't so bad after all. "Please," I said, using all my tricks—the tears, my pain, her love.

And it worked. Dory slowly crawled in between the sheets. I settled her head against my breast and gently stroked her hair. We lay together in this exquisitely safe place for a long time. Finally I said in a quiet, gentle voice, "Baby, you're letting your imagination run away with you."

And Dory whispered, "I guess so."

GRANDDAUGHTER: "Only women stir my imagination," wrote Virginia Woolf in the perfect naming of my muse. Like the poet Hilary Stevens in May Sarton's novel *Mrs. Stevens Hears the Mermaids Singing*, the men in my life "nourish" me, but it is only the women who "move and shake" me.

I have always loved women. Chased women, lured women, been cowed by some, and intimidated others. Succumbed to their charms, traded confidences, trusted and feared women. Toward women I have felt desire, surrender, competition, contentment, hatred, curiosity, and love. My hottest passions and bloodiest cruelties have always been with women. Women, for me, are both endlessly remarkable and infuriating. With men, too, I have felt love, as well as lust, intellectual passion, and indifference. I have never been indifferent toward a woman.

As a child I watched Nana sit on the edge of her bed wearing only her girdle, a large flesh-colored garment built from cloth, bone stays, hooks, and ribbons. She'd lean over, pendulous breasts grazing knees, and bunch up her nylons, slowly pulling them up over fleshy thighs, to the dangling hooks of her garters, where she'd flick aside the coy ribbon and catch the fabric between the soft rubber backing and its chrome anchor. Then she'd say, "Hook me up, sweetie." And I would slowly thread each small metal hook into its proper eye, up the long row, hook by eye by hook by eye by hook.

That done, we would move into the bathroom, the inner sanctum of all that was secret and female. There I would sit quietly on the closed toilet seat watching Nana as she put on her face, shaking out a small puddle of foundation, rubbing it into her neck, my eyes anchored to the lifting of her finger, the arc of her arm. Then she would say, "Here, turn to me." And I would. And she'd dip her finger into the rouge pot and dab a bright spot on each cheek. "A big smile now," she'd say and I'd grin as she rubbed the pink until it lay soft against my skin.

I have always dreamt of the soft bodies of women, and have slept their hot, sweet love since my mid-twenties, starting with ephemeral affairs indulged on trips away from home and my live-in boyfriend, dalliances charged by the energy of the stolen, the illicit, the clandestine. Later, after leaving this man, I was seduced by the romance of being a woman in a world of women: separatist dykes who loved fiercely and danced bare-breasted at parties on Halloween night. A furious, passionate, defiant community of women that replicated my mother and grandmother's intimate universe, albeit roomier and less venal. In that world I met a different kind of Mother, embodied by Adrienne Rich and Audre Lorde, mothers who cultivated mindfulness and political commitment, encouraged independence and nurtured the soul.

Grand Rapids, Michigan, 1977. The site of my journey from the general to the particular, from loving the community of Women to loving one specific woman, Q.: passionate, brilliant, stubborn as myself, and rumbling with life.

We lived in the bumblebee house, a converted single-family residence painted yellow and black, humming with female industriousness. I nested in the attic apartment, preparing the classes I taught at the local experimental college and worrying *Daughter Rite* into life. Coming off of the sixties, I also "experimented," meaning I slept with anything that had two legs and moved: men, women, men and women.

On the first floor lived Q., a truck driver for AT&T, the first woman in Michigan to storm that particular male stronghold. She'd stagger home after a twelve-hour shift, exhausted from fighting the iciness of both the male truckers and the cold Michigan roads. Chilled to her marrow she'd jack up the heat, causing me, living under the eaves, to roast. I'd pound on her door, stripped down to a T-shirt, demanding that she lower the heat. She'd smile, turn the dial down, and once I had left, flick it higher than originally set. A struggle of firstborns, evenly matched.

Winter thawed and so did our relationship. We spent the spring rocking on the front-porch glider, dishing the dykes who believed working class equaled stupid, sharing girlfriend pointers (I was smitten with my first serious relationship with a woman), discussing books, and falling in love. It was her way around language that hooked me. I, the college professor, talked like a hick: short choppy words, limited vocabulary, simple declarative sentences. Q., the truck driver, spoke poetry. She assessed the hum and buzz around us with a nimble mind, describing people and situations with tight, exquisite phrases that were at once perceptive, witty, and metaphoric. Word upon word, she demonstrated the power of language to tip the universe a fraction of an inch, revealing a breathtaking view. I was seriously earnest; she made me laugh.

Q. embodied a startling complexity: tough enough to hold her own against the male truckers withered by her presence, yet soft enough to peer into my heart and breathe "Come." Q. built a world in that house that I cautiously entered with both my mind and my body. A womanly place, but valenced differently than the place of my childhood: spacious, joyful, and large-hearted. For the first time in my life I felt at home. I was completely satisfied and knew I would never be satiated.

GRANDMOTHER: I was clipping on my earrings when Jack walked in. I gave him the once-over and told him to change his tie, there was shmuts on it.

"It's fine," he said.

I picked up the tip of his tie and held it up to the light. "Hurry up and change it," I told him. "We're late."

"So we'll be late. Stop telling me what to do."

But I couldn't stop. "Someone has to," I said. "Go change. I won't be seen with you like that."

"Enough already," he said as he shuffled out.

I shouted after him, "And while you're at it, change the shirt."

"Stop nagging me!"

I gave myself the final once-over. I hated my dress. I went to find Jack.

He was standing in front of the open hallway closet in his undershirt. I looked at his soft belly and told him, "You've gained weight. Wear the blue shirt."

Jack came at me. "*Shut up!*" he screamed and hit me across the face.

We stood there, just staring at each other in shock. I wondered who was going to speak first. I remember hearing the clock tick, and far away, someone leaned on a horn. And then, from somewhere deep inside me bubbled up, "This is not a life."

Jack answered way too fast, "It's fine," and walked away.

"No. No, it's not. Listen to me." Jack was buttoning up his blue shirt, his back to me. Nothing could stop me now. "Talking to you is like talking to a wall," I said. "Stop fidgeting and look at me." Something in my voice must have surprised him because he turned. I was too tired to care. The words slipped out. "I was wrong," I said to him. "I thought I knew better, but I didn't . . . What did I know? I was so young."

And my husband said, "I don't know what you're talking about."

I told him I was talking about me and Nate. Me and him.

Jack turned away and I grabbed him. "I was flattered by Nate's attention. I admit it. But what about you?" He says nothing. "I hate you," I scream at him. And still he says nothing. "What is it? The money? We made a pact with the Devil and we became demons."

"I don't know what you're talking about," he says again.

"If you don't, gotenu, there's no hope for us."

He understands. For the briefest of moments I see a pain in my husband's eyes. And then . . . it's just gone. Vanished. "You're meshugeneh," he says. "I did nothing wrong."

"Just this once," I plead with him, "don't let your pride run your life. Please. I'll never beg again."

Jack looks at his watch. "We're late," he says. And he walks out, leaving me standing alone in the room.

GRANDDAUGHTER: As a woman artist I have always worked from that place where the erotics of my muse and the erotics of my body coincide. To say it another way, both my muse and my love for women spring from the same source—my complex relationship to the Mothers of my childhood, both in my relationship to my mother and grandmother as individuals, and in my relationship to them as an intimate couple.

As a child, I watched my mother and grandmother sitting so close that when they inhaled their bodies touched. Often it was impossible to see where the skin of one ended and the other began. This felt dangerous, as if one would drown in the flesh of women. Yet it also drew me to it with its promise of intimacy, affiliation, empathy. From their world of oneness, alienation and isolation were forever banished.

They talked quietly together late into the intimate night and helped each other in small, daily ways. Nana was diabetic and each morning my mother would clean her own mother's flesh with an alcohol swab and then pierce her skin with a needle carrying lifesaving insulin, an act both life-giving and intimate, which felt, to me, covertly sexual. My grandmother, in turn, listened to my mother with a focused empathy that understood, held, soothed. Their relationship was more alive and vital than any relationship I saw either of them have with men.

But I'm idealizing here. As a child I hated their relationship and their tight bond that excluded me: the natural needs of a "selfish" child *and* the cries of a child whose abuse is unseen. Their relationship was symbiotic, claustrophobic; its lack of boundaries was terrifying. Neither would make a decision or enjoy a moment without the other one sharing in it. It seemed that only when seen, heard, and understood by the other could an experience gain form, become real. Where did my mother leave off and my grandmother begin? Where did I?

With my imagination and my body I enter into this spinning, twisting, female space, to reexperience and understand my relationship to the mothers of my childhood. It is through both my art and my love for women that I puzzle through the irresolvable contradictions imprinted by my particular mother and grandmother. This is my psyche's itch, which I scratch with my art.

GRANDMOTHER: Let me tell you a story.

An old woman sits in a room and she sews by hand with tiny stitches a small dress meant for a child. There's a pile of such clothes on the floor beside her. There are also jars of dried leaves and flowers on the table in front of her. Whenever a baby is born into the community, a member of the family comes and announces it to the old woman. The old woman silently listens and then nods her head. After the father or mother or aunt leaves, the old woman takes a dress off the pile, sews on a pocket, and fills it up with leaves and flowers. Sometimes she sews it at the waist, sometimes on the sleeve or at the back of the hem. Each dress is specially made for each child. Once a child was born with a bad deformity; she would never walk. The woman sewed leaves in the neckline of the dress destined for this child. As the child grew older she began to sing and with each year her voice became more beautiful. She was the most famous singer the village was ever to know. Another time, the woman sewed a few flowers into the sleeve of a dress for a different child. As she grew up, her arm shriveled up and became useless, even though she was born with perfect wholeness and beauty. Once I went to visit this old woman. She was an ancestor of mine through my mother and her mother and hers. She lived in England near the trees and I knew she was a powerful witch.

GRANDDAUGHTER: Did I have a deformity when I was born?

GRANDMOTHER: You were born into this family.

GRANDDAUGHTER: Did you sew a pocket on my dress?

GRANDMOTHER: Yes.

GRANDDAUGHTER: What did you sew in it?

GRANDMOTHER: Rachmones, my special one. Compassion.

GRANDDAUGHTER: My mother was raped by her older brother in the twenties, starting when she was eight years old. I was raped by my grandfather in the mid-fifties, starting when I was about five. My mother and I, each in our own isolation, shared an ugly and cruel fate. And the silences of our memories kept us apart. My mother's inability to remember her own incest abuse meant she couldn't protect me. My inability to remember my incest meant I couldn't forgive or understand her. A troubled mother-daughter relationship was built on the secrets we each held buried. We both finally remembered. First my mother, and then me. But remembering, telling each other, could not easily change the patterns of thirty years. That is the paradox and the tragedy. Both my uncle and grandfather are long dead and my mother and I stand and face each other across a gulf dug deep by the actions of these two men, a gulf that we can't easily bridge, may never be able to fully bridge. One lifetime might not be long enough. I love my mother and my mother loves her daughter, but there is a closeness denied us. My mother can't bridge the gulf because her own incest created a need for intimacy, and her own mother's death created a vacuum that I can never fill. I can't because my mother's needs resonate too shrilly off the violations of my body's boundaries that I experienced so young. I have intimacies in my life, deep intimacies, many with women, but not with my mother.

I do, however, make movies. I create melodramatic films that put the audience into their bodies, memories, and lives; emotional films that make them as vulnerable as I am as I create them. Where the audience and I meet in the emotional space shaped by the film, a kind of intimacy lives. An idealized mother-daughter relationship, one that I long for yet could never tolerate with my own mother, is what I create with my films.

I don't know if Nana knew of her daughter's and my incest. My mother says she never told her mother about the repeated rapes by her brother. She steadfastly insists that she didn't want to turn her mother against her only son. I also suspect she was too terrified to speak the truth, truly believing that if she did so she would die as threatened by her brother. Nana, entangled in her own drama, could save neither my mother nor me. Remember, this was fifties America, before the second wave of feminism, before our understanding of the power and abuses of the patriarchy, before our awareness and speaking out against the violence perpetrated on women and children, before battered women's shelters, and rape task forces, and sensitivity training for police. My grandmother was a woman of her time who, understandably, saw few options.

GRANDMOTHER: The sky is ominous with low hanging clouds. The water of the Atlantic is white-capped, whipped by a strong wind. The breakwater of rough-hewn granite boulders lining the shoreline barely holds the water back from the land. The stacked granite looks like huge steps leading down into the water. People are everywhere: teenagers pet each other on the rocks, families picnic in the shade of a few trees, fishermen stand with their lines disappearing into the waves.

I sit on the breakwater as far away from these people as I can. I rest on the lowest boulder, my feet dangling in the water. As the wind whips a spray up over the rocks, I turn my body to catch the full sting of the cold water: my left shoulder, my right arm, my face.

I remember being fourteen years old. I wanted to bleach my hair, to be a modern girl. But Mama said no. That surprised me. Mama never said no to me, but she did that day. It made me just furious. No one would tell me what to do. Not even Mama. I ran out of the house and poured a bottle of peroxide on my hair, a bottle stolen from the drugstore. Then I marched right down Main Street, through the center of town in the Labor Day parade for all the world to see. When I came home Papa smacked me across the face. But I didn't care.

GRANDDAUGHTER: There is no ending to either Emma's or Anne's story, no dramatic climax or closure. I view her as a child would her mother. Although I try to possess her, and do to some extent by telling her story, I will always be the child. Much is hidden. Much is silent. She is unknowable. Mysterious. Ineffable.

My mother and grandmother's working-class lives were fraught with dominations and deprivations, both economic and sexual. These experiences, filtered by their particular psychologies, vibrated through their lives very differently. I always believed that my mother was overwhelmed by the pain of life while Nana held the pain, lived with it, never denied it, yet also never succumbed to it. Compared to my mother, she was the more seductive figure.

I have always romanticized my grandmother and, by comparison, disparaged my mother. Nana defied conventions, or so it seemed to me, by aborting three pregnancies, then engaging in a twenty-year affair. She eventually quit her job and spent her mornings watching *Queen for a Day*, while in the afternoon she played poker with her crony friends until her death at age seventy-two. All the while my mother, devoted to her own mother, expressed her womanhood by chauffeuring my grandmother to these afternoon games.

But I don't want to end here, with the bad and good mother still left intact. With my mother patronized and my grandmother romanticized, her actions whitewashed as an antidote for the dark image making of the mother in *Daughter Rite*. Both my mother and grandmother, in their own ways, mothered me well. Together they gave me the skills I have needed to live a life full of love and work, in which I have thrived.

When Nana died, my mother finally left home. At age fifty-seven, she moved to Hawaii, where she worked for twelve years as the secretary and bookkeeper in a prominent gay male bar and restaurant. She vividly showed me that you can always change your life: it's never too late, you're never too old. My mother devoted her years in Hawaii to helping young gay men who had AIDS. She put her immense energy into fundraising, cooking dinners for men whose own mothers had rejected them, listening to their fears, standing vigil while they died. She is the most kindhearted and nonjudgmental person I know. From her I learned to open my heart.

My grandmother had different lessons to teach. Eva Hoffman, in her book *Lost in Translation,* describes the adults who surrounded her during her complex childhood growing up as a Jew in Poland just after World War II:

> I am haunted . . . by the idea . . . of the normal. The normal, in my mental ideogram, is associated with a face. . . . It's a face that has seen a lot, and is not easily astonished. It knows, in its cultural memory, the limits of human ideals, and the limitations of human passions. . . . It has a stored knowledge, passed on through generations, of the devious traceries of the human heart, and it has learned where the mean lies in the soul, and what's excess. The normal is derived not from a conventional norm but from this knowledge of proportion. The face expresses a skepticism that's a hair's breadth away from cynicism, but is also adjacent to an acceptance of things as they are, and not as they should be or might be in a more ideal, a nonhuman, world.[1]

Nana had this "knowledge of proportion" and an acute understanding of what it meant to survive life. Neither of my mothers rescued me, but Nana, caught in her own complex drama, was a companion in negotiating a life filled with contradictions and paradoxes, sexuality and power. With her anger, feistiness, and strength, she guided me by example through the difficult times of my own childhood. She showed me that living with the full knowledge of your contradictions gives you, perhaps not an easy life, but certainly one of dignity and empowerment. Although it has taken me half a lifetime, I am finally learning her lessons. She taught me how to live with my eyes open, she taught me how to see.

GRANDMOTHER: Stop it! You didn't love me because I was heroic. I was selfish and hard. Face it, you loved me because I loved you. I was the queen bee, but I was your queen bee.

GRANDDAUGHTER: I adored you.

GRANDMOTHER: Because I protected you.

GRANDDAUGHTER: Yeah, except for one thing.

GRANDMOTHER: What?

GRANDDAUGHTER: I was raped by your husband.

GRANDMOTHER: But I did protect you. You needed to believe there was someone in charge. Someone minding the store. I gave you that.

Necessary Fictions

Today, I am not sure that what I wrote is true.
I am certain it is truthful.
:: Charlotte Delbo, *Auschwitz and After* (1995)

The Story in 1988 . . .

They sit together and talk around death. He is only fifty-five years old and he's dying. pH 7.45, PO_2 48 on 60 percent O_2, PCO_2 28, BiCarb 18. Their strange language echoes off the metal conference table they're squeezed around, perching, slouching, shifting in the plastic form chairs that fit no one. In this gleaming teaching hospital—rooms glass-walled for easy observation and little privacy, cinder-block corridors dressed up with the happy primary colors of children, a place of heroics and action and do everything imaginable but do no harm—these young doctors are scared. I sit ignored in the corner, watching. I sense their fear.

This is one of the secret pleasures of being a filmmaker—you get to be the voyeur. Ride the ride as a quick thrill. Feel the feeling without owning it. As I and my two film colleagues have been doing, every Tuesday for the past few years, observing the afternoon discussion of patients on the intensive care unit in this big city hospital. We're researching a film on high-tech medicine, staying at the edge of the action, silently witnessing as the medical staff struggles against disease's chaos with their hard-edged experience, secret tongue, and dark humor.

I love hanging at the hospital, eavesdropping on the doctors' conference prior to their visiting the patients en masse. Valuable information on the condition of individual patients is shared, different programs of treatment are assessed and weighed. During the discussion that unfolds, the interns and residents learn from the more experienced attending physicians, whom I secretly think of as Daddy Doctors. These daily conference rounds are usually led by the head doctor on the unit, a cardiologist I've come to admire. With penetrating questions, he inches the young doctors toward diagnosis, treatment plans, and knowledge. As physician and teacher, he displays a finely tuned sense of the contradictions inherent in his work, which he meets head-on with compassion and irony.

I respect these young men and women. And at the end of each Tuesday, I go back to my sedate academic life, leaving behind the uncertainty and ambiguity of trauma, disease, and death. That is another filmmaker privilege: you get to walk away. But today something different happens.

Today for some reason there is no Daddy Doctor to lead the conference rounds, no one to mind the store. The attending physicians are all otherwise occupied and the young interns and residents must step into the adult shoes of the absent father and discuss the patients among themselves.

The patient they're discussing is a fifty-five-year-old upright family man, white and educated, married to a loving wife. He could be their father, or worse, their future, for they are mostly young white men sitting around the table today. It's their identification with this particular patient that motivates what happens next.

The patient is gravely ill and the young doctors express doubts that he will live out the week. This is one of the worst possible situations. They want to help, they've been trained to help, but they can't—medical training hasn't adequately prepared them for death. The young men are impotent against death and their rising anxiety fills up the room. What makes them even more distressed is the exact nature of the patient's disease: AIDS.

A young male intern presents the patient to the group, rattling off the facts of the case, which he reads from the white index cards clenched in his fingers. "He figured he had asthma. On admission an HIV test proved positive. A CD4 count of forty-nine. He's suffering from PCP, Pneumocystis carinii, and CMV, cytomegalovirus. He's being treated with a Bactrim drip and . . . and . . . ganciclovir. Breathing's difficult. And he's not conscious." The intern flips over the card. Only blank whiteness. There are no more facts to carry him forward. He looks up and shrugs.

Into the silence, a young male resident drops the question they're all thinking. "He says he's straight, right? Then how the hell did he get infected?"

The intern looks back down at his cards: the answer's not there. So he speaks from his remembrance of his history-taking with the patient. "Says

he went to some wild parties between his first and second marriages. Said at this one party he remembers getting smashed and passing out . . ."

"Yeah, sure, got it up the ass and never woke up," chuckles another male resident.

"More like he liked it and went back for more," says another, playing to his audience.

That cracks them open. Nervous giggling erupts around the table. Defensiveness dressed up in cruelty. The sharp edge of their homophobic laughter slices me where I live. I slouch deeper into my corner, shrinking in size. There is no attending physician to halt this appalling talk and I feel personally attacked because of my own queerness, though none of them know that I'm queer. What's worse, the patient they're talking about is a friend of mine, although I haven't realized that yet.

The discussion ends and the young doctors file out into the corridor. They will now walk around and visit the patients they've been discussing. It is time to meet face-to-face with the flesh and blood folk who embody the medical data scrawled on the white index cards.

I take my time leaving the conference room, hesitating in part because I still sting from their cruel joking and in part because I never feel comfortable coming face-to-face with the patients myself. I'm not a physician, and even though I'm always introduced to each patient and only stay if they grant me permission to do so, I've never overcome the feeling that my presence is somehow inappropriate. In the convoluted dance between very ill people who desperately need help and physicians who try to heal despite their limited powers, I, the filmmaker, am superfluous. This is the dark side of being a voyeur, one reason why it feels perverse.

I pack up the tape recorder and go in search of the herd of doctors. The tail end of the blue coats is just now veering off down a side passage at the end of the hall. Walking toward them, I round the corner and see in the distance A., a friend I occasionally meet for dinner and a movie. Strange . . . what's she doing here, I wonder as my mouth goes dry and my knees turn watery. In the thump of a heartbeat, a lock deep in my unconscious quietly clicks open and a fragment of knowledge floats up from the depths: it is A.'s husband the residents mocked. It is A.'s husband dying of AIDS. His name was spoken during the conference rounds but my brain, either denying or confused by the strange context, did not properly sort the information. Knowledge I didn't know I possessed blindsides me in a swirl of recognition and disbelief.

The corridor recedes in a whoosh, like Hitchcock's famous *Vertigo* shot, leaving a dizzying nausea in its wake. I gulp air in a desperate attempt to hold down a sudden, humiliating need to vomit. The bright-colored cinder-block wall shores me up. One of the young male residents peels himself off the end of the line and hustles over. He asks if everything's all right. I nod yes. Knowing better, he gently guides me into an empty room, sits me down on the edge of the bed, and lowers my head between my legs. He instructs me to breathe deeply. The vertigo slowly evaporates. He asks what's wrong and I assure him that I don't know what brought on the dizziness, but I'm fine now. Mission accomplished, he trots back to the authentically ill.

As soon as he's gone, I bolt into the small bathroom that adjoins the room and vomit. I hug the toilet all the while, telling myself how inappropriate and irrational my behavior is, but I can't move. My pounding heart pins me to the floor of this quiet, cool place. It slowly occurs to me that what I'm experiencing is terror. I cautiously taste the feeling with my mind. Dread. I probe deeper and touch the certainty that I know something I shouldn't and will be punished for my knowledge, a reaction way out of proportion to a slight dizzy spell. Rationally, I take stock of all the secrets I hold, as if listing could harness the terror. The information cuts both ways. I know what my friend A. doesn't know—the disrespect, born of anxiety, that the young doctors flung at her husband in the conference rounds. And I know what the doctors don't—that my friend's husband is bisexual, a fact and the consequences of which A. has shared with me often. I conclude that I've been dizzied by the swift and astonishing slide from voyeur to participant, from safety to danger. But what danger?

Panicked, I puke again.

After a while, who knows how long, I push off the tile floor and

splash cold water on my face. I step out into the corridor. A. stands at the far end, her back to me. I command my feet to walk the thirty-foot distance to my friend. When she turns, relief sweeps across her face. I am one of the few people to whom she has confided the secret of her husband's sexuality, someone who requires no explanations. We spend the rest of the day and much of the night sitting on the edge of hard hospital chairs; she talks, I listen.

Four days later A.'s husband dies. Hundreds of people attend the funeral. Her husband was much beloved, an important benefactor to cultural and social institutions, a supporter of the arts. Many people speak of his compassion, his generosity, his intelligence, his humor. No one speaks of his AIDS. It is the unacknowledged, the elephant in the living room. I'm enraged at this silence, obsessed for weeks with the lies and hypocrisy of the funeral. Once again, my response is flagrantly out of proportion to the situation, not to mention at odds with my usual sensible self. This I know. But it's as if some evil, screaming demon child has risen up from my core and no analysis, no rationalization, can still her tantrum.

And then the dreams come. Worse than the nightmares that followed my mother's confession of her incest.

I wake up every morning dreaming of death. In one dream my mother dies, in another my father, in yet another my sister. In most of these dreams, men threaten, rape, and then kill me. Sometimes it is my sister who is threatened, but I outsmart the men and take her place, and only then am I raped and killed. I die again and again each night, surrounded by death.

My days, tightly structured with work, serve to blot out the nights and the ever present anxiety that corrodes my insides. This ability to ignore the body's message, to live life through the mind, has been sharpened to a fine edge against the hard stone of my childhood. I've been granted my long-ago childhood wish to stand safely behind the camera, the director of films and of life. It makes me invulnerable, or so I think. Nowhere is this more evident than in my relation to Q., my companion, the great love of my life.

By now we've lived together ten years and patterns have been set. My job is to keep the material world spinning efficiently around us: to pay the bills on time, to balance the checkbook to the penny, to organize our meals. Q. is in charge of the emotional housekeeping. All that is traditionally feminine—vulnerability, intimacy, surrender—the qualities owned by my particular mother, I shun. Instead I leave this feminine sphere to Q., whom I love precisely because she embodies these qualities. I want to be near them, but not to own them.

This thins my life down to an existence barely nutritious, a kind of weak emotional soup. Independent and self-sufficient, I fix the broken garage door and chase fame while Q. sits on the couch, highly literate in the silent language between two bodies at rest. I, unable to read this foreign tongue of the body, get bored. It all boils down to hand washing. Q. leans over the sink and soaps the palms of her hands, her fingers, her wrists. She performs this cleansing like a Buddhist practice, thoroughly engaged, as if the mere act of hand washing holds the possibility of transcendence. I, on the other hand, splash on the water, give the soap a quick slip-slide over the largest surfaces, all the while calculating where I have to be next. If Q. lives in the hidden depths of the moment, I run five minutes ahead, straining to catch up with myself but never getting there. I am very efficient, waste not a moment, accomplish a lot. But I savor nothing. Remember nothing. Feel nothing. Perhaps this is the point.

Teaching. Students. Faculty meetings. Hospital observations. Film meetings. Social engagements. Phone calls with friends and my sister. Q. Every minute of my waking is used up and there's not enough time. I spin life like a top, faster and faster, defying the pull of gravity.

A dread of secrets consumes me. What secrets? Whose secrets? I rifle through my mental files. My friend's secret of her husband's AIDS? My mother's secret of her childhood incest? My grandmother's secret of her twenty-year affair, which I, as a child, hoarded as one would a precious fetish?

Secrets, lies, and betrayals swirl around me, angry ghosts that are sensed more than seen. "We dance round in a ring and suppose / But the Secret sits in the middle and knows," writes Robert Frost.

Then one morning walking to work I can't catch my breath. In pig-

headed denial, I climb the three flights of stairs to my office just to prove that nothing is wrong. I finish the last flight by pulling myself up by the railing, hand over hand, step by labored step, doubled over, gasping for air. That night as my breathing grows ragged and anxiety mounts, Q. tries to take me to a hospital. I flat-out refuse to go. But she is a persistent and crafty soul. She sits with me through the night, with one hand laid on my back, the other on my chest, and minute after minute, hour after hour, she paces her breathing to mine, imperceptibly slowing us both down until my fear abates and I'm willing to accept help.

But I gloss the story, polishing the truth to a flat luster.

The day actually started at my analyst's office in an old, brick building near the university where I teach. My analyst is my female Other: married with children, upper class, WASP. But all this is superficial because what I feel in her presence are the qualities of my grandmother: passion, fierceness, intelligence. For eight years my analyst has minded the store while simultaneously inching me toward trust and intimacy in the hope that, once experienced within these safe walls, they will bloom out into my life.

Her room is tiny and safe. There are objects everywhere: nature photographs and abstract prints on the walls, Native American fetishes and bowls on the shelves. My analyst is particularly fond of the bowls. Being a Jungian, she believes in holding the feeling—the anger or anxiety or terror or shame—and what better metaphor for vesseling than a bowl?

There is one particular bowl that always pulls my gaze. The outside surface is as brown and rough as dried, caked earth, the inside as smooth as glass and very dark. The bowl's shape is bulbous, fat and round at the middle, sharply tapering at both the base and the top. The mouth of the bowl is so narrow that light can't easily penetrate the interior. It is dark inside. A secret place.

Feelings, as usual, are safely boxed away this day. The conversation stalls. My analyst glances around the room. Her eyes settle on the bowl. "What if you and I got in the bowl together?" she asks, crafty and smart. "How would that make you feel?" A therapist's game that we've played before.

I fantasize about slipping into the bowl with my analyst, its deep darkness wrapping around. Claustrophobia slides in behind us and catches me off guard. Breathing becomes rocky. My trusty escape mechanism efficiently clicks in and detaches my head from my body. Uncomfortable feelings recede behind a thick glass wall and words pour into the emotional space left vacant: Drowning. Anxiety. Fear of intimacy. Control. I speak them all. I pretend at being a person who can feel. When my hour is up I leave, not realizing nor betraying just how crushing the panic. But my body will not be denied its cry. In the ten minutes it takes to walk from her office to mine, I lose my breath and my health and I can't find them again for two years. Literally.

In the hospital that night, I am diagnosed with adult-onset asthma. I simply reject the news. It's impossible that I have a chronic, potentially life-threatening illness; I'm as healthy as a horse. Vegetarian. Daily yoga. Swimming half a mile four times a week. Even aspirin never passes my lips. This asthma attack is a slight inconvenience that will pass like a summer cold. It takes two more middle-of-the-night trips to the emergency room to finally accept the inevitable: that at age thirty-nine life is irrevocably changed.

And despite the medicines of both East and West—the teas of comfrey root, mullein, coltsfoot, and lobelia; the pills of theophylline and cortical steroids; the inhalants of cromolyn sodium and albuterol—the asthma cannot be controlled. The doctors are puzzled; I am scared.

When health departs, energy tags along for the ride. Insufficient breath is exhausting. I fall dead tired asleep at nine o'clock only to have constricted air passages jar me awake, panting for breath, forty-five minutes later. A couple of puffs off the inhaler relaxes my lungs and calms my heart. I drift off to sleep only to shudder awake after another forty-five minutes, clawing once again for air. This cycle repeats itself all night, night after night, until the memory of a full night's sleep is beyond my imagination. With no air there is no sleep. With no sleep there is no energy. With no energy there is no life. I lie on the couch all day staring out the window, not even thinking. Breathe in. Out. In. Out. Occasionally, on a lucky afternoon, I slip beneath the surface into a brief nap.

Do you want to know what asthma feels like? Go find a plastic coffee stirrer, the slender hollow kind, usually brown or red, that is used to mix in sugar and cream. Place it in your mouth, pinch your nose closed (don't cheat), and breathe in through the stick. A small dribble of air flows in, so slight in volume it can't possibly satisfy your need. You reflexively suck harder, thinking that will and pure force can draw the air in. All it does is lock closed the back of your throat, choking you. Then comes a coughing spasm, your body's reflex for dislodging whatever is blocking your airways. It's your own inflamed passages that are the obstruction, though, and coughing only seizes them more, draining your last pool of energy, making you faint.

You try to relax while panic bleeds through, killing any hope of relaxation. You think you can outsmart the straw by sipping the air in a slow, steady stream. This works for, say, twenty seconds, before the lack of oxygen forces you back into deep sucking. Which, of course, is useless.

Tears fill your eyes from the frustration of struggling so hard for so little. Your lungs hurt from the lack of oxygen. Imagine a ten-pound sack of flour sitting on your chest, a sack that you must push up and down with each breath, the pain growing deeper, the breathing more labored. That's part of asthma, too. The strange pain that comes, not from your body surface's harsh contact with the world, but from deep within yourself. Life shrinks to one thing: breathing. Every ounce of strength you possess, every bit of concentration you can muster goes into managing a process that the rest of humanity takes for granted. You helplessly watch as your life shipwrecks on the hidden shoals of your body.

After a few months my body adapts. Sleep visits for as long as two hours at a stretch. With careful planning, I can accomplish one thing a day: have a brief meeting with a student, teach one class, return maybe two phone calls. There is nothing left for a social life. There is precious little left over for Q. The noise in my life has ceased and in the stillness I hear the roots of my psyche quiver.

It is then that the elephant makes its first appearance.

I dream: My father is holding my hand, I am a child (although strangely, it is a dream father by my side and not my real one). We are about to turn a corner and he says, "I want to show you my elephant." I don't want to look. He says, "Don't worry, it's okay." I'm scared to look, but I can't help but peek around the corner and catch a glimpse of the elephant. It's gray and huge. Out of her mouth comes a long, thick thing. She's vomiting up this thing. It looks like a fur ball that a cat would vomit up. It looks like compacted garbage covered with mucus. It looks like an engorged penis. I think, "Oh, her asthma."

Upon awakening, the dream reminds me of Susan Pitt's short animated film, *Asparagus*, a mischievous work that imagines the vegetable in every conceivable domestic space: lurking behind the living room curtain, rising out of the bed, dropping like shit from a woman's bare ass into the swirling pool of a toilet bowl. These asparagus, with their slender stocks and enlarged tips, announce the female character's fluid desire for the penis: alternatively exhibitionist and voyeuristic, coy and lusty. In recalling this film, I gain a glimmer of dream understanding about the elephant standing in the living room of my unconscious. My elephant embodies both the male and the female, a "father's" penis and a daughter's asthma, the two inexorably linked by my psyche. The fact that a penis-like image rests at my dream's core rattles me. I have, after all, avoided the real thing for more than a decade.

I sink further into my illness. It is a familiar space.

I've visited here before. Eight. Twenty-one. And now thirty-nine. Three moments of contained madness in what has always felt like an otherwise unremarkably beige life. Convinced that if I can discover a pattern my asthma will fall under control—the comforting mind-over-body security of illusion—I focus on an agent outside myself: drugs. It's a drug, I reason, that each time set my life askew.

Reserpine. Ovulan 21. Prednisone. Three drugs prescribed and consumed just prior to my three episodes of craziness. At eight years old I was diagnosed hyperactive and given reserpine, a drug commonly used in the

fifties to calm hyperactive children. Now known to cause depression, it's rarely prescribed. Is this why I wanted to kill myself at eight? A drug-enhanced depression? Then at twenty-one, a doctor prescribed Ovulan 21 for birth control. Within three weeks, I had slipped into a severe suicidal depression, a risk for a small number of patients taking this hormone. And now I'm thirty-nine. Early in my illness, an emergency room physician gave me prednisone, a steroid with anti-inflammatory properties that is used to treat many illnesses, including acute asthma. It's a powerful drug and, judiciously used, it saves lives.

I resist the doctor's advice: drugs scare me. But the attending insists that four days on prednisone isn't going to kill me. I acquiesce to his judgment and within twenty-four hours I have plummeted into the deep black pit of despair. Prednisone, like all hormones, can have emotional side effects. Some people experience euphoria; a small percentage react with debilitating depression.

Eight. Twenty-one. Thirty-nine. A pattern of drug reactions. But unsatisfied—only an airtight case will do—I search for additional evidence and find stress.

At thirty-nine, I play out my overscheduled life of relationship and work against a background hum of emotional unease: nightmares first triggered by my mother's incest revelation that have intensified with my friend's death, and the cold, humiliating fact that I haven't completed a new film in six years.

The most recent film, *What You Take For Granted . . .* , a film about women—working class and professional, African-American and Caucasian, gay and straight—in traditionally male jobs, was completed five years ago. If *Daughter Rite* is a film about my relationship to the Mother, both my particular mother and the symbolic Mother, *Granted . . .* is about the daughter's relationship to the Father. If *Daughter Rite* is emotional, passionate, intense, *Granted . . .* is the opposite: sociological, cool, detached. I'm convinced that the film, with its disassociated feelings and disembodied talking heads, is a failure: aesthetically and professionally. Viewing it causes such inner turmoil that I've canceled trips to wondrous places—Moscow, Saint Petersburg, Tokyo, and London—unable to tolerate the anxiety provoked as the film's images flicker across the screen.

I'm in an artistic nosedive and the ground is coming up fast. The medical film was the last of many attempts to save my career with a new project. It almost worked, lasting three years and spawning the beginnings of a real film. But that too has crashed and burned in the heat of my illness. I suffer an artist's worst fear—an extinguished creative fire.

Then there was twenty-one, a year so strained by the upheaval of graduating from college and my forthcoming marriage that I had wanted to die. And what of my suicidal desires at eight? Silence. Whole years of my childhood are mysteriously mute, secluded behind a thick muffling wall. The question of why an eight-year-old child would want to kill herself haunts me, the great, dark beast that lurks on the far side of the wall, formless and menacing.

Still I dig for patterns, hoping to solve the puzzle of the present, and in doing so, resolve the puzzle of the past. I conduct an archaeology of the body. A disease has shaped each breakdown. At eight I couldn't shit, at twenty-one I couldn't eat, at thirty-nine I can't breathe. These symptoms define a barrier between my body and the world, a ruptured boundary that has been slowly occluded by damming up my ass, closing my mouth, and shutting down my lungs. Holding on, not letting in, not letting go, my body over the years has gradually sealed itself off from the world. I imagine this "thing," unknown and unnamed, creeping up the landscape of my body, from the bowels to the stomach to the lungs. From my ass to my mouth to my nose. It can't go much higher, I reason; soon its journey must end.

Another asthma attack. Another trip to the ER. We've learned the best hospital to run to in an emergency: the one that lets Q. sit by my side while we wait the five hours until the drugs do their work and breath returns. There is something soothing about hospitals. During the two years of my illness, I never felt as safe as when lying on a gurney in the brightly lit emergency room, Q. holding my hand, the nurses bustling around, keeping us company at three in the morning.

Asthma, and its repercussions, is a self-consuming and internal

process. Many friends flee from my overt neediness and dependency. A few, besides Q., stick with me for the long haul.

My analyst stays committed to me and to our process. She keeps a tight frame around our room and minds the store, a rock-steady presence that I home in on as she reassures me that there will be an end to the darkness, even if it's hidden by the murk of my mind. There is also my best friend, an internist turned psychiatrist, who responds to every medical panic without judgment. She helps me negotiate the intricacies of the medical world that are beyond my experience. More importantly, on days when Q. goes to work and I'm terrified of being alone, I rest in her presence while she steeps us tea and helps me sort out the twisted corridors of my psyche.

There are also the acquaintances who pass through my life, unexpectedly touching it, like the graduate student, a woman from India, who brings me home-cooked meals in Tupperware containers. Exotic, tasty foods laced with ginger to settle my stomach. She literally feeds my hunger and by doing so, my heart.

But mainly there is Q., with an empathy as wide as the oceans, which swells and lifts me as the whirlpool of feelings threatens to suck me under. Middle of another long, hard night. I sense the calling of my name as a low vibration undulating through the thickness of sleep, pulling me up from the depths of the nightmare that has me entangled on the bottom. I swim to that voice, rise up and bend toward it. Breaking the surface of sleep, I hear Q. gently calling my name. She tethers my anchorless self to the land and selflessly lets me just . . . be, not knowing when, or if, I'll return back to shore.

My ever present need to regulate and direct my life grows to monstrous proportions. Q. humors my need to control the dust, control the air, control what we eat, what we drink, where we sleep. Her generosity and good humor carry us along, but the unacknowledged contract of our relationship has been shredded by my illness, revealing a deep fault in our dynamic. Asthma and its turmoil have forced me to neglect my material world responsibilities. I check out and Q. assumes the grueling work of the physical world and then some. She shops, cooks, launders, and even cuts work to chauffeur me when I'm too ill to drive to the doctor, the shrink, my classes. And still, she minds the emotional store, while I revel in my distractedness.

Our relationship of perfect equipoise wobbles. Audre Lorde, in *A Burst of Light,* writes about her own struggle with illness "that sometimes we cannot heal ourselves close to the very people from whom we draw strength and light, because they are also closest to the places and tastes and smells that go along with a pattern of living we are trying to rearrange."

Independent and dependent, yang and yin, masculine and feminine, butch and femme, good girl and bad girl. Opposites might attract, but they don't coexist peaceably over the long haul. With illness I have become dependent without really understanding how to be intimate, while Q. has come up against the hard reality of her own dependency, which understandably shakes her. Neither one of us confronts this directly, but the ground no longer feels solid under our feet. Our passionate and caring relationship has always been peppered with land mines, buried since childhood. Q. carries a rage, banked low, that can flash flare and which I, encased in my hard shell, can easily deflect. Her anger blows, my defenses harden, and we freefall into knock-down, drag-out emotional explosions where we mutually, verbally abuse ourselves and each other. In my most honest moments, I fear that I need our fights. Only such explosions can test my defenses and reinforce the belief in my saneness. When we fight I can feel, if only anger and fear.

And then the elephant appears again.

I dream: I'm holding my dream daddy's hand. I feel safe. I see the elephant and we walk toward it. I clutch tighter. "It's okay," my dream daddy whispers. We walk right up to the elephant and my dream daddy indicates that I should stand still. The elephant sniffs me with his trunk: my face, my neck. I pull back and squeeze dream daddy's hand tighter. I know he wants me to stay. The elephant sniffs. His trunk glides around my neck and down over my shoulder and chest. It moves between my legs and rubs my geni-

tals. It excites me. This feels good. I hold on tighter to dream daddy. His
trunk continues to rub and tickle. I become scared, confused. My body is
jittery, yet my hand that squeezes dream daddy is warm. I squeeze tighter, it
will keep me safe. I don't like this anymore.

I awake in the middle of the night, coughing uncontrollably, choking, pulse racing, drenched in cold sweat. I suck on the inhaler every half hour, but it's still not enough. I tiptoe downstairs so as not to disturb Q. I slip on the stairs and face down, thump, breaking the glass of water I hold and badly bruising my elbow and thigh. I crouch on the stairs and in loud, throbbing pain, weep. Q hears me. Finds me. Changes my wet nightshirt and comforts. I go into the downstairs bedroom to sleep and walk into the doorjamb. Accident-prone I look down at my body—it's covered with purple bruises.

The next day is spent lying on the couch, too listless from the lack of breath to think, too agitated from my life-saving drugs to sleep. The asthma has done its job, distracting me from my dream's message.

And then my doppelgänger knocks on the door to awareness.

I dream: I'm searching for Michelle, who is me. She can't be found.
I suspect she's dead since I hear rumors that she has fallen into the water.
I wait almost breathless for news, too scared to search for myself. A
woman lifts up a plank floating in the harbor. "I found her," she yells out.
I look. Michelle lies on her back in shallow water that covers her. Her eyes
are closed and I think she's dead. They pull her from the water and lay her
on the ground. Her eyes are shut but her chest moves slowly up and down.
She's breathing. "She'll be all right," someone says. "Just let her come to.
Then you can speak with her." Later Michelle visits me. "You have to tell
me how you survived so long under water," I say. She smiles and pulls a
child's sheriff's star off her shirt. "Here. See?" She bends the shaft of the
pin straight. She puts it in her mouth, tilts her head back and breathes.
Then she laughs. Ah! She used the pin as a breathing tube so she could
breathe underwater all those years. How clever.

This dream is seductive and strange. There are two of me: crafty and dumb-witted; active and passive; heroic and weak; alive and dead. My contradictions materialized through my two bodies, the binary opposites endless. Is this my doppelgänger, the demon I must fight? Or perhaps this other Michelle is the Prince who will wake my Sleeping Princess self? Yet in another contradiction, it is the sleeping one who knows. During one fitful fragment of sleep, I dream that I'm holding a young girl child in my arms. As I lay her down, I accidentally twist her body and it breaks apart at her waist. Break-away baby. The young girl child is now in two halves. I'm quite agitated. No one else seems to worry.

Frantically, I try to control the spiraling chaos. There is a small green notebook. Down the left side of the page are scrawled the hours of the day, across the top, the days of the month. Every time I suck on my inhaler I draw a little line marking the exact time; two puffs at once make a cross-hatch. A visual calendar of breathing. There are also descriptive notes: bad wheezing, lump in throat, someone sitting on my chest, two-hour coughing fit. I urge the scratches to speak their secrets. I count the marks to discover that I've sucked on my inhaler fifteen, sometimes twenty times a day, an excessive dose that signals danger. Even with that, on top of all the other drugs I consume, the asthma won't be controlled.

Fearful, I refuse to take prednisone. I can't breathe. I can't sleep. I can't eat. I float on the couch, cast adrift from my life. I do not leave the house.

At twenty-one I slept around the clock to avoid my demons. Now, eighteen years later, I barely sleep in an attempt to evade my dreams and their knowledge. Ever vigilant, insomnia triumphs. But insomnia is an inadequate word. Sleep disruption is more precise. Imagine being roughly shaken awake every hour or so. You become desperate for sleep but nothing tempts it. The slide into oblivion deserts you. There is no rest. You feel continually disoriented, nauseous, and dizzy. Concentration is impossible. (The three nights I slept a continuous seven hours during my five years of insomnia are emblazoned in memory as small triumphs followed each time by a day of delicious clearheaded energy.) Without sleep, the border of the

unconscious is ruptured and the repressed seeps through the cracks in your defenses. You live in a free-floating state of nerve firings and random associations. You live in a liminal space between sleeping and waking, between dreaming and flashbacks. Where is the line between fantasy and memory?

Where is the line between panic and asthma? Where is the line between illness and madness? Where is the truth?

In the dark hours of the night when sleep eludes me, writing gives solace. And slowly, insidiously, I am lured by its promise. Frustrated by its ignored messages of body and dream telling, my unconscious chooses my art as its vehicle of revelation. I start writing a script for a new film, called *Pandora*. And in the hush of night, my buried self rises up from my unconscious to greet me as I read on the flickering screen the words I have written the night before: that it is me and not Dora, my grandfather and not Jack, who are the characters of the incest story I tell. A memory? An imagination?

Where is the truth?

Another middle-of-the-night terror. Pounding pulse. The 3 A.M. red glow of the digital clock. An odor: dirty male genitals with an over-smell of stale urine. The odor fills my nostrils and snakes down my throat. The strong taste of semen. Like Pavlov's dog responding to his dinner bell, I start salivating and can't stop. I lie stiff, hands pinned to my side, the smell filling my face. The odor can't be real, I don't smell. Garbage. Food. Perfume. Nothing. I can walk into a house reeking of garlic and have no idea what we're having for dinner. The metal taste in my mouth makes my stomach lurch. And then a memory slams into my consciousness, clear and vivid: my grandfather's gas station, the back room with its toilet and small cot . . . oral sex.

A waking dream? A hallucination? A memory? A flashback?

Where is the truth?

I'm terrified of night. Afraid of what I might dream, might remember, might imagine. Exhaustion finally forces me onto the bed. Biting anxiety. Shortness of breath. Alert. I lie on the small cot in the back of Grampy's gas station. Scratchy old army blanket. Smudged gray walls. Smell of oil and gasoline. Scummy toilet. And the naked women. Naked women prancing across calendars and tool advertisements, gazing down on me. My body goes into spasms. Uncontrollable tears flow. Anger ignites up from the depths of my soul and consumes my body. Fury burns. I imagine sticking my fingers into Grampy's mouth and tearing the flesh from his cheek. I dig my fingers into his eyes, scooping the squishy balls from their sockets, as Nana tore the eyes from the whitefish before plunging it into the roiling water. I rip Grampy's head off with my bare hands, shredding muscles, bursting veins. Blood spurts everywhere, covers my hands, drips down my wrists onto the floor. I plunge my arms into his split flesh up to my elbows. A hallucination? A desire? I need to kill. Instead, I stomp around grabbing old *New Yorker*s and phone books and shredding them up, a trail of white paper tears marking my passage through the house.

The flashbacks join with memories. The dreams meld with flashbacks. Perhaps some or all are seasoned with a pinch of imagination. This doesn't compromise the truth of what is revealed. The secret is laid bare—and it is not the secret of my friend's AIDS or my mother's incest or my grandmother's affair. The secret unveiled is my own story of incest. I confess to my parents and sister and cousin in tearful phone calls. They are loving and supportive. No one disbelieves. Some have remembrances of their own.

But there is no magic bullet in either medicine or the psyche. Remembering does not quiet my asthma. The disease, wild and untamable, still grips me. The story unfolds.

For two years the doctors poke and prod, searching for my asthma's underlying cause; there usually is one when the disease suddenly erupts in an adult who never suffered it as a child. The doctors investigate the space of my body: swallow tests, motility tests, GI tests. They find nothing. Then someone thinks to look inside my head.

I wait patiently in Dr. P.'s examining room. He strides in wearing lizard-skin cowboy boots and an ego jammed into overdrive, smiling a big howdy. I like him immediately: a good-natured, take-control kind of Daddy. Dr. P. threads a long, slender optic scope up through my nose and delicately probes my sinus cavities, which have been transformed into a

world grown wild with polyps. He slips my CAT scans onto the light box. "Ah," he says, pointing here and there with the tip of his pen, "the disease is widespread." I read the film and see that where the black spaces of my sinus cavities should be, there is only murky gray. He advises aggressive treatment: surgery.

The surgery is not without risk. It's impossible to tell from the x-rays how deep the infection grows. Dr. P. rattles off the possibilities: one in two hundred patients goes blind from the close proximity of the optic nerve; also, the infection may have already eaten through the bone that surrounds my brain and he won't know until he gets in. Two years of playing the voyeur on the ICU floor has schooled me well. I ask smart, cool questions laced with the occasional medical term—prognostic factors, treatment modalities, protocols—so he'll know I'm not a dolt. More than anything, I need to be treated as an equal, not a patient. More than anything, I want not to be vulnerable, to have some control.

I leave his office and find the nearest pay phone to call Q. My fingers tremble as they punch in the number. When she says "Hello," I burst into tears.

I embrace the surgery, the symbolism of which enthralls. Medically it's described as endoscopic sinus surgery with bilateral sphero-ethmoidectomy and maxillary antrostomies with intranasal cryotherapy. To me that means going in and cleaning out the unnamed "thing" that has crept up my body, *Psychosomatic illness* slowly over the past thirty years, from my bowels through my stomach to my lungs, this "thing" I now name as incest.

The incest, spreading its own somatic song, has visited the various sites of my body's invasion: my ass, which was subjected to repeated enemas as a child, and I suspect abuse as well; my mouth, which was a favorite site of my grandfather. Now, at the moment of surgery, it'll be excised through an orifice that wasn't defiled: my nose. If the repressed has spoken through its special language of symptoms—feces, food, air, and my body's inability to process these basic elements of life—there is a symmetry and closure to the sinus surgery that is pleasing. My body, invaded by one Father, will be cured by the removal of the disease by another Father.

I decide that surgery is the procedure that will cure my body, and that when it's over I'll try hypnosis, a procedure I hope will cure my soul.

I agree to the surgery, but only under a local anesthetic. Dr. P. warns that very few patients can tolerate it. I am adamant. I will never again close my eyes to a physical invasion by a Father.

The night before the surgery, Dr. P. visits on rounds and asks me to re-consider my decision to use only a local. I don't budge. He assures me that I'll be given a sedative cocktail, a mixture of drugs that will eliminate the pain as well as relax me. He teases that the cocktail contains a strong am-nesiac and that I won't remember a thing of the surgery. I, of course, re-member every detail.

I remember winking like a coy mistress to Dr. P. as he entered the op-erating room. I remember the pressure of steel instruments scraping against bone, followed by the sound of bones crunching as the instruments broke through. I remember matter-of-factly telling Dr. P. that he had a huge ego, quickly followed by his resident joking, "I wouldn't say such a thing while he's inside your head with a sharp instrument." I insist it's an observation, not a criticism and anyway, it takes one to know one. The nurses and resi-dents titter; Dr. P. roars with pure pleasure. We discuss food and cooking, his favorite recipes and mine. We chat away like two old friends over lunch, while Dr. P. goes into my head with forceps and knives, cutting out the diseased tissue like he's plucking flowers.

The disease is endless. I inquire about the color and to my surprise Dr. P. answers, "Rosy pink." The next time he uproots a polyp from my head I ask to see it. It dangles from the forceps held just above my eyes. "See," Dr. P. says, proud as if the disease were his. It looks like a deflated, castrated penis wiggling helplessly from the tip of the forceps. I think: "He's removing all the penises from my head."

During the surgery my nose, the last orifice of my body, is penetrated as I keep my eyes open. For two hours while tissue is cut, bone is broken, and sexual imagery abounds, I look into Dr. P.'s eyes and signal, "Anything you dish out I can take and I want you to know it." <u>Standing behind the camera of my own life's story, I direct.</u> I am the heroic other Michelle of my

doppelgänger dreams, the privileged patient observing the secrets of doctors, the voyeur of my own pain and trauma. My curiosity at what's being done to my flesh is perverse. <u>I am unanchored from the earth and from my body, the queen of dissociation</u>. It's a strategy I have used to get through the dentist, a fight with my lover, the sexual abuse. A double-edged skill. *splitting*

The day after surgery, pumped full of antibiotics, steroids, asthma drugs, and painkillers, I float in bed stoned and uncomfortable. The pain sharpens, so I swallow my dose of codeine and drift off to sleep. Suddenly I bolt upright, heart pumping, gulping the air. Dread sweeps through my body and death hovers. I punch at the nurse's call button. A disembodied voice drawls that she'll be there shortly. I huddle in absolute terror, clutching the call box. Every nerve ending is firing. Nerve endings I didn't even know I possessed are firing. I punch at the button again. This time I demand, "Get. Here. Fast." I wait, eyes closed, to be rescued. Images appear. A lizard with sharp teeth rising out of the mud. A huge snake coiling to attack. Hallucinations. I know they are drug induced and will pass. Simultaneously I'm trapped in the delirium and want desperately to jump out of my skin.

The nurse materializes in the doorway. "Yes?"

Still self-diagnosing, struggling for control, I tell her it's probably a drug reaction but I'm in trouble and need help.

She asks if she should get the doctors.

"How the fuck do I know?" I scream.

She flees. The doctor comes. A twenty-five-year-old boy who stands at the foot of my bed leaning stiffly against the wall, as far away as he can get in the tiny room.

I try to reassure him while simultaneously pleading for his help.

He says, "Stop the codeine. The feelings will pass. There's nothing I can do."

I know that, goddamn it. Step toward me, my eyes plead. Hold my hand. Sit with me until this terror passes. But unprepared by his training, he's incapable of such simple human kindness. Infantilized and embarrassed in my patient state, I'm incapable of asking. The classic medical standoff. He flees the room.

I call Q., "Get me out of here." Within an hour or so, the panic passes and Q. arrives. When I enter my home, my body relaxes into its safety.

My sister arrives for a visit and she and Q. watch silently as I ramble through the house like a specter. My nose is stuffed with surgical packs, forcing me to breathe exclusively through my mouth, which is more terrifying than the surgery since breath now holds my deepest anxiety. Just before entering the hospital, I purchased a big leather reclining chair; strangely (though not really) it resembles the chair in my analyst's office, a chair I've sat in for years, groping my way toward trust and intimacy. It is only in this chair, sinking into its yielding leather, that sleep sometimes blesses me.

Ten days after surgery the packs are removed from my nose. They float in the green kidney-shaped tray cradled in my lap, limp-looking like used and bloodied tampons.

"You're healing just fine," Dr. P. announces proudly. "I do good work, don't you think?" I look up into his twinkling eyes, a kind Daddy Doctor, and suddenly there is something I must tell him.

Dr. P. looks down at me, waiting. My mouth opens to speak, but no words come forth. He waits. Waits. Patiently. "When I was a child," I say, "I . . . was sexually molested." Tears flow. He places his hand on my shoulder. Silence.

"I'm glad you told me." More silence.

There's nothing to add, the conversation fizzles. Dr. P. finally rescues the moment. "Did you know that the tissues in the nose are similar to those in the genitals? They're both influenced by the same hormones. When sexually aroused," he goes on, "both the genitals *and* the nose engorge with blood." And here's the punchline. "When you have too much sex in a short amount of time your nose gets congested. It's called honeymoon nose. Sometimes bride's nose."

I'm entranced. Another metaphor that captures my imagination, leading me out of my body and into the safe space of my mind.

In the days following surgery I feel alive, alert even. The shrouding

sickness has been cleanly excised by the surgeon's knife. Only now is the mess that surrounds me visible. The debris of my childhood. A film career in shreds. The disintegrating relationship with Q.

Illness sucks all the available energy into its hungry vortex. Two years of all-night vigils, emergency trips to the hospital, intense caretaking, and constricted life have finally worn down the relationship. Q. confesses that she's been having an affair. She's in love with another woman. She will, however, stay another year and nurse me back to health. I am too numbed by the news to argue.

The surgery helps, but does not cure my asthma. I cough endlessly. Not a delicate clearing of the airways, but deep, uncontrollable coughing fits lasting for two hours or more, leaving me red in the face and completely exhausted. The muscles between my ribs spasm from the strain.

Working my way through Daddy Doctors, I visit a chiropractor twice, both times ending up in the ER within a few hours of treatment. Convinced it's his fault, I weave a paranoid fantasy in which his therapeutic heat treatments, rather than relaxing my muscle spasms, have damaged my lungs. Afraid to return to his office, I'm equally afraid to confront him. I make and break appointments at a furious rate. Q. suggests that perhaps he's abusive. Physically he resembles my grandmother's lover, while his personality echos my grandfather. Click. Bravely, I call and confess that he reminds me of the man who sexually abused me as a child. He's professional and understanding. I never see him again.

My asthma spirals out of control, which is seemingly impossible. In one week alone I have two acute attacks. The doctor suggests self-adjusting my theophylline dosage upward, but cautions not too much: there's a fine line between therapeutic and toxic levels. The increased dosage does nothing. This is particularly worrisome since my hypnosis, with a woman, is scheduled at the end of the week, an appointment with destiny that I don't want to delay. My analyst discourages me from the hypnosis, believing that the psyche will give up its secrets in its own time, or not. But I, the doer, the director, am too impatient to wait. If possible, I would jackhammer the secrets loose.

I up the theophylline dosage again despite the doctor's cautions. My reward is a pulse closing in on one-fifty and the creeping dread which that signals: panic attack. And still there's no air. I goose up the drug dosage again and trigger yet another panic attack.

I rush to the ER, terrified of my self-destruction. The ER physician reads my chart with its two-year story of uncontrolled asthma and promptly admits me. I'm back where it all started: in the teaching hospital where I researched the medical film. Except this time I am the patient, not the filmmaker, the exhibit not the voyeur.

At the first set of doctor rounds I still perform my customary role: the one in control. All those Tuesdays spent on the intensive care floor of this very hospital in which I now lie have prepared me for this moment. The doctors don't intimidate; instead, literate in their tongue, I charm with my bantering knowledge of medicine. My reward is being labeled a "good" patient—articulate, funny, bright—and being treated as an equal.

The rounds are led by Dr. L., an attending physician in pulmonary medicine. He, and not the pulmonist I regularly see, was the doctor on call the night of my admission. It's just as well. My own doctor is my age and has been acting like a brother when what I'm looking for is a Father. Dr. L. fits the role perfectly: older, New York sharp, and tough-minded. I loathe him on sight.

Dr. L. listens as an intern presents my case. He quickly scans my chart and decides on a course of treatment: prednisone. Unlike my regular pulmonist he can't be dissuaded. We negotiate hard. He opens with sixty milligrams.

"Twenty," I counter. "They make me hopelessly depressed."

"Thirty. Anything less just won't work. And I can give you drugs for the depression."

"Twenty," I plead.

He looks me straight in the eye and says, "You can die with asthma as out of control as yours. I don't care how long it takes or how long you stay in this hospital. You are not walking out of here until you deal with your asthma. You decide." His gaze does not waver. I've finally met someone

with a will as strong as my own, a Father I can't charm. A Father who minds the store. I acquiesce to the thirty milligrams of prednisone.

Two A.M. Heart pounding. Pulse racing. The nurse calls the resident on duty, who stands sleepily at the foot of my bed and says like he's reading a menu, "Panic attack, it will pass, just relax," and walks out.

Left alone, bereft of human warmth and kindness, I ball into the fetal position of a frightened child. Every nerve in my body is charged with a feeling so intolerable that I need desperately to escape my skin. I slip out the IV and stand at my tenth-story window with the certainty that jumping is the only relief. The nurse finds me there, trapped by modern architecture's sealed windows. She leads me back to bed and gently reinserts the IV. The panic fades and in its place rest only shame and humiliation.

My ego has fled sometime during the long night of panic and irrationality, stripping me of the last defenses, leaving only a child in my place.

At rounds the next morning, this child grasps at adultness by chastising the young resident for his callousness during the night. Dr. L. admits he was wrong about the prednisone and prescribes a different steroid, one he suspects won't have the same psychological effects. He turns to leave and the desperate eight-year-old child I have become grabs the tail of his gray coat in her fist and tugs.

Puzzled, Dr. L. turns and looks expectantly. I am struck mute. Pulled by the silence, he sits down at the edge of my bed; the rest of the herd quietly shifts in their shoes. I, or rather this eight-year-old I that has infiltrated my body during the harrowing night, blurts out, "He put his thing in my mouth." Seven simple words uttered by a child. I wait for the sky to come crashing down, the world to slip off its axis. Nothing happens. No cataclysm. No whirlwind. No annihilation. I cling to this man, this doctor, this Father, and sob. He sits quietly, respectfully, and in the fullness of the emotional maelstrom just . . . is.

Finally he says, "I'm glad you told me. It explains a lot. I think you'll be fine now."

I've finally cast the right doctor into the role of the Father. The father who must know. The father who can hear. The father who will rescue. And

I have finally written this father into the right scene: a hospital, glass-walled for easy surveillance, with cinder-block corridors dressed up with the happy primary colors of children. A public place of no privacy where it is safe to speak of my abuse. Like the child in the fairy tale, I have uttered the magic words to the right jinn. The spell is broken; from that moment my asthma is controllable. Even more, the deeper curse has snapped; the black demon of my soul vanquished.

That night I'm hit by a cacophony of emotions—grief, relief, humiliation, joy—that collide, pair, break apart, and reconfigure, tossing me into the air with great force and then setting me back down, softly, onto the earth in a place I had not known existed. A ground of inner calm not even imagined. I have missed the hypnosis, scheduled for the previous day, when I overdosed myself into the hospital. My unconscious, and not my ego, had reigned, choosing the time and place to speak its secrets: to a father in a public hospital of sickness, not a mother in the private therapy room of hypnosis. Why a father and not a mother? I can only surmise that, unable to be rescued by the strong and powerful mothers of my childhood, I turned, in hope, to a father. This is ironic. I, who aping the Father have valued only the ego, have been healed by the canniness of the unconscious, that teeming ocean of desires and hidden agendas, perhaps the true director of life.

There is one more significant moment.

In the hospital I'm roomed with a beautiful young woman with flesh made large and doughy by dosages of prednisone so high she lies dazed night and day, drifting in the unquiet twilight of hormones. We haven't spoken a word to each other in the four days we've lain side by side in our square room. What I know about her I've learned from eavesdropping through the flimsy polyester excuse for a privacy curtain that is pulled between us: what the doctors would describe as "27 y/o bl woman w/severe flare-up of lupus."

My last night in the hospital, drifting off to sleep, I hear on the other side of the curtain, "No! I don't want it!" Then the squishing of rubber-soled feet across soft tiles.

"It's just oxygen," says the nurse, whose presence is marked only by an accented voice and the curtain's flutter as she moves invisibly to help my roommate.

My roommate lets escape a small wail, "It'll cover my face . . . I'll smother."

"Just these two small prongs that fit into your nose. See? It doesn't cover your face."

"I don't want it!" Bustling noises and I imagine the nurse bending the slender tubing to fit comfortably just inside my roommate's nostrils, where they will gently blow their life-giving oxygen. "I . . . can't . . . breathe!"

Then the doctor, whose presence I hadn't deduced, says in the loud, imperious voice often employed for imbeciles and the sick, "You'll be fine as soon as you get the oxygen." My roommate lets out a soft sob, which the doctor answers by telling the nurse in his efficient, clipped tone, "Give her three liters," as he sweeps out past me, into the flow of corridor traffic.

"Relax," says the invisible nurse, "you'll be fine now. I'll check back with you as soon as I can." Then the nurse leaves too.

From behind the curtain my hospital companion swallows tiny gulps of air. I sit up in my bed listening, afraid to go to her aid, afraid not to. Small whimpering sounds start to accompany the breathing gulps, beating out a rhythm of panic that is not unfamiliar. I slip off the bed and quietly part the curtain that separates us.

My roommate sits at the edge of her bed, hunched over and scared, the oxygen tube threaded under her nose, made useless by her gulping mouth. Her panic is palpable; it moves me. I shuffle over to her, clumsily pushing my IV stand at my side. When I arrive at her bed, she doesn't, or can't, acknowledge my presence. Lost myself, I sit down next to her. She is hyperventilating now, her whole body trembling.

I tentatively touch her arm. She stiffens slightly but says nothing, neither does she pull away. I lay my open hand on her upper back, over the place where I know her lungs flutter. She closes her eyes and leans into my touch. I, too, close my eyes and pant, matching my breathing exactly to her quick shallow gasping. Slowly, imperceptibly, I quiet my breathing down.

She unconsciously paces herself with me, her breathing becoming deeper and slower with each breath she draws. Her shoulders relax, her face softens, tension slips from her muscles. I lift my hand from her back. She turns and smiles, thank you. I nod an acknowledgment and slip back behind the curtain to my own side of the room. The next morning she is gone.

changes .. ' Q., and illness, have taught me well. I've fluttered my emotional baby wings, flew into the bowl and experienced intimacy with this stranger—precisely what I avoided with my analyst and denied Q.—and discovered ease and quietude.

I leave the hospital and return to my disintegrating home. It takes only a few months to completely collapse into rubble. Q. decides to move out. My illness has alerted her to the need to build a life of her own, separate from me. After two years of touching me as helper to my healing, she is going to take care of herself. Q. offered humor, nurturing, safety, and love. When she left my heart crumbled.

Work, too, has crumbled. There are no film projects left for me to return to. I reinvent myself as a writer, a foolhardy choice since my craft lies in images, not words. Yet in the act of writing, the Michelle-who-stands-behind-the-camera steps out from the shadows and joins the little girl who, long ago, paraded up and down the sidewalk for Daddy. And in the quiet solitude of writing, I feel my way to a long desired conversation with myself, across the decades, between different Michelles. Not that film can't enable such conversations, only that the loudness of machines, the army of people, bright colors, strong sounds, big close-ups on huge screens, often *control vs. vulnerability* drown out such delicate talk. Through film I donned the mantle of the Father, ambitious, successful, detached, controlling, all-seeing, but circumscribed, too. By stepping out from behind the camera, I moved into the more vulnerable position of the one looked at, scrutinized, seen. The one who feels.

In the act of writing, many points converge. I never felt comfortable with language. Perhaps the inability to utter the most important word of my childhood—incest—made me wary of all words, for what use was language if it couldn't communicate the essential thing that needed to be said?

Perhaps my insecurity with language is banal, rooted in my eight-year-old breakdown, which caused me to miss much of the third grade and the foundation of spelling and grammar, which was taught that year. Perhaps it is simply an issue of class. The language I learned in my childhood home is a dialect distant from that of the academic world I inhabit. There are moments, even now, when I speak and, in the cold silence that follows, I realize I've mispronounced or misused a word learned from a book, never heard. The act of writing sits at the intersection of the incest, class, and my strivings to leave my family behind. Ironically, writing leads back to them and to my self. Through writing I claim history and self. In the words of Gore Vidal writing in *Palimpsest,* I could "not possess my own life until I had written about it."

autobiography - publics?)

I move out into the world. It is not a conscious decision: rather I find myself being invited to parties, and going. Being asked to dinner by new acquaintances, and going. It's spring, the third spring since asthma entered my life. Two years of self-absorption and worldly withdrawal. Two years in which I broke apart, then reconfigured. It is a different Michelle who ventures out into the world. For one thing, I'm always worried about what to wear. The old Michelle never cared. Now nothing seems appropriate or comfortable; the new Michelle hasn't yet found the persona that, inevitably, clothes signify. For another thing, her taste in people has changed.

I lunch with friends. There is a woman there, a stranger. We are both aware that this is a contrived meeting so we can eye each other in the safe company of friends. She's bright, witty, interesting. She tells stories that are simultaneously entertaining and smart. I long for intimacy with this woman. That moment of the unexpected, when your eyes meet and if there are words, they're just ephemeral, fragile conveyances that carry the feelings across the space between two bodies. These words between us are different. I actually see them tumbling into the vacuum, filling it up, building a thick wall between us. This wall of words protects us from each other, makes intimacy impossible. Our interaction is empty and tiring. The old Michelle never would have noticed or cared. The tragedy is that I've learned this lesson too late for Q.

My sister and I go on a pilgrimage to our grandfather's grave. We drive for miles along Centre Street as it winds through the Boston boroughs of Jamaica Plain and West Roxbury, through crowded shopping districts and strangely desolate stretches. Finally we come to a row of cemeteries set across the street from a forlorn-looking tract of ranch houses.

"Hand-in-Hand Cemetery 1875."

We park off the road, half on the sidewalk, or what would be the sidewalk if there were one. We walk back to the entrance and through the rusted iron gate. An old, dilapidated house hugs the outside fence. Perhaps the caretaker lives there and will provide a map so we can find the grave.

The front door has no bell, nor a handle to open it. My sister knocks at the back door, but no one answers. A man's shirt, frozen in a grotesque shape, flaps on the line. Off to the side is a shopping cart filled with empty aluminum cans and lumpy garbage bags. There is a single narrow path that leads back through the graves.

My sister and I walk down it. The gravestones are tightly packed, one against another, on either side. The poor who lived in tenements in life are buried in tenement-like closeness in death. There are no trees, only headstones. This is a place to warehouse dead people; there is no pretense.

My sister spots the headstone that marks our grandparents' grave next to the cyclone fence.

We stand in the cold, gray day and stare at the mottled, metal-gray stone. I silently beg for a flash of memory, insight, anything. What I get is feeling: I'm profoundly upset. My sister puts her arm around me.

"I don't know what to do," I say.

"Put a stone on their grave. Leave our mark so they know we came." I fish a small stone from the rubble at my feet, as does she, and we place them on top of the grave. I take a photograph: a material memory. We leave.

One day, soon after, I notice that I have long fingernails, surprising since I've nibbled them my whole life, a nervous tick. As a child I gnawed so much that my mother painted my nails with pepper-laced Vaseline, but that didn't stop me. As an adult my chewed fingertips were embarrassing,

but even that didn't stop me. Getting asthma did. Suddenly I have new hands. And in other ways, too, a new body. My hair grows long and I buy the first dresses I've owned in twenty years. I move more slowly through the world. I notice birds, how their heads dip for seed and their legs fold as they take flight. I spend hours and hours alone in the house or sit solidly in the present talking with friends. I've even started, when washing my hands, to just wash. I believe that I will never again fall prey to the dark, creeping devil of suicide and that certainty creates a deep peace I've never before experienced. I don't work nonstop. I learn how to play.

The story is . . . I've been sexually abused as a child. *what is the truth?*

The Story in 1980 . . .

I am thirty-one years old.

In six weeks I will step onto a plane, buckle myself into the seat, and go hurtling through the sky for the eight-hour flight to Berlin, where *Daughter Rite* will be shown at that city's international film festival. The trip is weeks away but already my stomach cramps in anticipation and nausea rises up, making me dizzy.

These over-the-ocean journeys are wretched since I have no choice but to fly. For the trips that cross hard land I ride Amtrak, first class, in a private sleeping compartment where I read and daydream and the phone never rings. In a life of collecting friends and tasks and responsibilities that fill up every possible moment, the train's isolation is a relief. I enter a small, self-sufficient room—bed, basin, toilet, chair, and window—and, for twenty hours, relax into its quiet.

When I was in college and freshly in love, my husband-to-be was awarded an internship at the Council of Economic Advisers in Washington, D.C. Every few weeks I'd hop on a plane and fly down to spend the weekend with him. My very first flight. Eighteen years old. As the plane banked in takeoff and Boston sparkled far below in the dawn sky, I felt cut loose from the earth's pull and everything else that bound me.

Try as I might, I can't remember the moment that flying turned on me.

Daughter Rite changed everything and took this working-class girl on the best ride of her life. First, there were the cities: Los Angeles, Santa Fe, London, Edinburgh, Amsterdam, and now Berlin. Places I had dreamt of but never imagined I would have the money to see.

There was also the excitement of being part of a <u>larger political movement—of both feminism and film</u>—from which I derived a sense of community and purpose. I became a woman filmmaker at a time and place, the early seventies, when many things about being both a woman and a film-maker were rapidly expanding.

And then there was the attention. I loved it. Admit, you would too. Who doesn't want to be asked serious questions, listened to attentively, publicly lauded. Even more important, the film made me a star in the milieu I cared most about: the world of intellectuals and avant-garde film. My attraction to this world was the clearest expression of my relentless upward mobility, pursued through the mind, not the purse.

Determined to rise above my working-class family by proving I was an intellectual, I made Art, not movies. Movies were associated with the cultural products that defined my childhood home—*Reader's Digest Condensed Books, Popular Mechanics, Queen for a Day, Mantovani's 101 Strings*—and bookcases that held tchotchkes, not knowledge. Art was the cleanest way to put distance between my family, who embarrassed me, and myself. Art was a tool of self-definition for a life they couldn't enter.

And then there was the sheer bravado.

Filmmaking takes muscle, stamina, and power. You hoist a thirty-pound camera on your shoulder, work sixteen-hour days, and command people, usually men. I was a proud woman in a man's world and it was not easy, which just added to my pride. There was, for instance, the famous male feature-film director, adored by intellectuals, who, following me on a panel, announced to the audience that the most important thing needed to direct a film was balls. His sly remark, directed at me—the only woman whose work was being shown at the prestigious international film festival we were both featured in—spotlighted the conundrum of my psyche. I was offended by his erasure, yet at the same time, his remark was precisely what attracted me to directing in the first place.

Treading the border between genders, I was both and/or neither masculine and feminine. Enamored with the metaphoric balls required and bestowed by directing, I obviously didn't own, or even want, the real item. As Anna, the truck driver in *What You Take For Granted* . . . , says, "I got this attitude that I could stand in shit up to my eyeballs and not let anything af-

fect me. You know, I was in my lock device. 'Cause I wasn't gonna let them scare me off. And that was good for me. I needed to do that."

Through filmmaking I achieved my childhood wish. I became the Father standing behind the ground-glass wall of the camera's lens. Since I have many other walls in my life—the wall of Art that separates me from my family, the wall of amnesia that hides most of my childhood—this is a familiar relationship to the world. Safely behind the camera, I observe instead of act, watch instead of feel. Or rather I feel, one step removed, through actors and images. I pour my feelings onto celluloid, not into relationships.

This, of course, creates tension in my personal life.

Timing is everything. The year before, Q. left her secure truck-driving job and moved to Chicago so we could be together. It is at this very moment that my career, thanks to *Daughter Rite,* takes flight. And I want, need, to take this ride. Q. hates my traveling because, for her, I'm never really home, even when physically there. On my side, traveling provides a break from intimacy, which, feeling dangerous, can only be indulged in small doses.

I announce the Berlin trip. The fight commences. She screams. I withdraw. She turns up the volume of her anger. I get more distant. Which makes her enraged. Which makes me rational. Which makes her the bad girl. Which makes me the good girl. And I need desperately to be the good girl.

Berlin beckons, and I wouldn't miss this trip for the world, but the thought of actually stepping onto a plane, buckling myself into a seat, listening to the engines rev, eludes even my imagination. My therapist suggests hypnosis.

The next Friday we arrive at the hypnotist's office. Dr. S. looks like a Midwestern minister: clean and tidy, and definitely gay. He explains that hypnosis is really just self-hypnosis, that I will remain in control at all times. We talk about my fear of flying. Then he asks me to close my eyes.

Dr. S.'s voice is gentle, steady, positively caressing. At one point he moves closer and shows me how to communicate kinesthetically with my fingers: wiggle the index finger to indicate "yes," the center finger to indicate "no," the ring finger to indicate "maybe."

Once I am relaxed, Dr. S. takes me on an imaginary plane ride: the calling of my flight number, boarding, the safety instructions, the takeoff, cruising, and landing. Then, his voice low and soothing, he asks if there's a reason for my fear of flying. I think, of course not. Immediately my body announces otherwise.

With curious detachment, I notice my index finger twitching "yes." Soon my whole body joins in: torso shakes, mouth quivers, tears pop through closed eyelids. The disparity between my mind's knowledge and that which my body holds is shocking. An earthquake moment, like when the ground, which should be rock solid, flows like water. A permanent shifting of the continental plates of your mind, violating and profoundly distressing.

mind/ body [handwritten margin note]

Dr. S. quietly asks if I've told anyone. My finger quivers "no." He strokes my hand and tells me to relax. "You don't have to tell anyone now, either. I hope you understand that." His voice, hushed and tranquil, drives the fear back down into the black depths of my unconscious. The ground grows firm. Emotional balance is restored.

Dr. S. gently asks if I want to work on the source of my flying anxiety. A finger shakes its answers, but even though it is my body, my finger, the answer is hidden from the "I" who speaks it. I surface up to normal consciousness. What happened is never mentioned by either Dr. S. or my therapist. Yet, reeling, I never forget it.

Disorientation nags at me for days. I'm aware of my two episodes of madness, at eight and twenty-one, locked away in a tight box labeled "not Michelle." Michelle is accomplished, responsible, successful in love, well liked and optimistic. The breakdowns hidden in the box are an oddity I've never examined too closely. Dark pieces of inner life, secured under a lid that approximates the front door of my parents' home: a lock in the knob, a sturdy deadbolt, two chains, and a smaller, sliding bolt positioned right at the bottom, in a place no thief would ever think to look.

Suddenly I'm curious. Why did I want to die twice in my life? My

question bounces off a wall thicker than time, impenetrable to my probing. Burning to see what lurks on the other side, I walk its endless perimeter, soundless and blank, only to bang my head against its solidness. Blindly, with the conviction of a true believer, I decide it's my grandmother's fault.

I make elaborate timetables. As Nana passed through menopause, she fell into a deep depression, waking up in the middle of the night screaming for death to take her. She was fifty, I was eight. Her emotional states were sympathetic vibrations that my body was tuned to and I decide that our connection was so seamless that when she craved death, I craved death. I'm convinced that my fear of flying began on the flight home to attend her funeral. This, of course, is wrong. Ten years later, while reading through my journals in preparation for this book, I discover that the plane ride that turned me was the one taken home for Grampy's funeral, not Nana's.

But in my mind it is my grandmother who's associated with death.

Nana's greatest fear was of being buried alive. She often told the story of her best friend from childhood, a young girl who became sick and died. At least everyone thought she died. They put her in the coffin, embalming not the practice then, and screwed down the lid for burial the next day. In the morning when the undertaker arrived he heard scratching noises coming from the closed coffin. The girl had awakened during the night and, frantic, was trying to claw her way out. My grandmother, terrified of the same fate, insisted that when she died the undertaker be instructed to prick the bottoms of her feet with needles. She also made my mother promise not to bury her for three days. This was contrary to Jewish practice, which requires the dead to be interred within twenty-four hours of death. My mother, the loving daughter, respected her own mother's wishes above those of the Lord.

The connection between Nana and me was borderless. I read her desires and obeyed, her companion through life's joys and her own suicidal panic. I follow my problems of intimacy back to my grandmother, who loved me selfishly, excessively.

The story is . . . I've been mothered too tight.   *what is the truth?*

The Story in 1969 . . .

Six chicks hanging in the dorm lounge draped over hard, square chairs, earnestly rapping about boys. And sex. I am one of the crowd.

Everyone's reading Freud in psych class and the urgent question is: do you have vaginal or clitoral orgasms? It's a trick question, though we can't articulate why since the feminist movement rattling toward us is still just a mumble. But we must sense a trap of some kind since we eye each other around the circle, waiting to see who dares to go first.

It's a tough lead; no one wants to fall short of being a woman. Finally one girl takes a deep drag on her cigarette, blows a perfect set of smoke rings and declares: only a vaginal orgasm counts, only that is mature, womanly sex. The ice is broken. We go around the circle, one by one, and tentatively describe what our orgasms feel like, sorting them into prized climaxes and hopeless embarrassments. Must your entire body pulsate? Does your asshole have to twitch? We finally agree that it only really counts if it happens when he's inside you. Climaxing any other way—like clitoral stimulation—is cheating.

I, alone, remain silent. I've had orgasms since fifteen, rubbing against the trousered legs of innocent boys, but this doesn't count. Technically I'm still virgin, so rare as the sixties close that it's embarrassing to publicly admit it. Especially since I'm engaged to be married. Especially since I'm creeping up on twenty-one.

A year earlier I had finally engineered my escape. After living at home and commuting to a downtown Boston college for my freshman and sophomore years, I applied to the private university that my boyfriend, C., attended, sixty faraway miles from home. I was accepted, but room and board, on top of tuition, was way beyond my means. The only distant college even marginally affordable was the old aggie school, UMass, the working-class university in a state where the kids with either brains or money attended Clark or Brandeis, Mount Holyoke or Smith, Amherst or Harvard. Tuition at the state university was two hundred dollars a year, which meant I only had to scrounge up money for a dorm room and meals.

My father agreed to co-sign a loan which I would work off while still in school. Cash in the bank, acceptance letter in hand, in August of 1968 my boyfriend, soon-to-be fiancé, drives me beyond the pale. As the car eases onto Interstate 90 and breaks free of Boston's suburbs, my new life begins.

My first achievement upon arriving at UMass was an act of reinvention. When my new roommate asked my name, I hesitated a heartbeat and answered "Michelle," snapping my link with Shelly, the tainted name of my childhood. Shelly—with her lank hair unwashed for weeks, her duck-toed slouched walk, her certainty that everyone was in on the joke but her—was buried in that moment of announcing Michelle. Michelle ma belle. My birth name, adult and worldly, which felt inauthentic, but which I hoped, by the mere act of assuming, to deserve.

Michelle road tested her new name all day and was never challenged. Emboldened, she immediately bought her first pair of jeans, clothing that Shelly had been forbidden to wear because "they're just not ladylike." Shelly, made to wear skirts even to bowl, always felt awkward; Michelle, in her jeans, would blend into the crowd.

This glorious first day of my liberation ended that night as I stood by my bed, pulled off my clothes, and slipped between the sheets buck naked. I flaunted my immodest behavior in front of my roommate, who discreetly undressed in the closet. Out of my childhood home at last, I let down my guard and slept nude in a dorm with one hundred other young women and felt no fear.

At UMass I turned myself into an A student while typing for minimum wage in a secretarial job I did every available daytime hour I was not in class. All that I'd hoped for had come to pass—intellectual stimulation, close girlfriends, a nice boyfriend, distance from my family—everything had clicked into place . . . until the weekend I got engaged to be married.

The emotional charge of that moment vibrates through time, though I have no recollection of what season it was or much else about the world

outside the car. I do remember that C. and I were stuck in traffic in his blue
Buick Skylark somewhere in Boston. But why we were in Boston that
weekend and not in his hometown or in Amherst is a mystery. Perhaps
what happened next had something to do with the fact that we were on my
family's home turf.

C. says something funny. I laugh. I remember that clearly, laughing.
His love cradles me in its warm cocoon. There's a pause and C. says,
"Let's get married." And thwomp, the thick glass wall descends, with me
safely tucked behind it. I glance over to see if C. notices, but he's only
driving. Sitting behind the wheel, eyes on the traffic, he looks to me like a
stranger.

C. grins at me, pleased with himself. We've known each other for
years, having been high school sweethearts since meeting in a national Jewish youth organization. Everyone—family, friends, C., me—assumes our
destiny is with each other. I have no reason to be blindsided by this moment. I had tried to marry this same boy earlier. Then my parents threw a
fit since we were only sophomores in college and they said way too young.
Just wait a year, they said. (Two years before that, while still in high
school, I had tried to move out, into an apartment with an older girlfriend.
They had nixed that, too.)

Last year I fought to marry this boy as though my life depended on it
and now, a short twelve months later, C. is once again asking me to be his
wife. Timing is everything and C.'s is way off. Instead of feeling the right-
ness of his offer, it's come too late. I know this marriage is doomed. But
this inner knowledge is ignored, overridden by a deep fear that has no
name but which is dulled by the presence of this young man—with him I
feel safe—and by what he represents: a permanent escape from my family.
And so I say yes, smiling and hugging him, telling him how wonderful it all
is. Which is a lie since I know with absolute clarity that I no longer love
this kind, funny, smart boy.

I rush back to my dorm after the big weekend and show off the engagement ring to all my friends: a one carat emerald-cut diamond with a
slight but invisible flaw. It seems befitting the situation. Everyone oohs

and ahs over my trophy and I am sort of happy for the first time that I can remember.

Now that we're officially engaged, C. wants to have sex. I resist, inexplicably frightened of intercourse. But he gently pressures me: it's the free-love sixties, we're in love, what are you worried about? I have no answer. Finally I cave in. The first night we "do it," whatever lyrical pleasure might be there is drowned out by a thunderous feeling: a terror of getting caught. By whom? Who knows? After a few months of sex, which I can't relax into, I miss my period and, in a naive panic, I jump rope all day hoping to induce a miscarriage. Out of sync with my generation, I'm pierced by the shame of having slept with C. before marriage. A month late, my period comes with gushes of blood and breath-stopping cramps. Wising up, I drop by the student health center for the Pill, the only senior among a throng of freshman and sophomore women.

I discover *The Feminine Mystique* and *The Second Sex* and the Redstocking pamphlets and Valerie Solanas's *SCUM Manifesto* and within this frame, marriage looms dark and obliterating. Since a wife's name is replaced by her husband's, I'm obsessed with the scenario in which, after my marriage, no one will be able to find me. I will vanish. I imagine friends visiting the city where we're to move after graduation. They'll look for me in the phone book and . . . they won't find me. Losing my name is an erasure. Death. This name thing is symbolic, but it feels quite literal, too. For in a few months, I will graduate from college and move a thousand miles away with my husband-to-be, away from my women friends, and a particular woman friend, whom I cannot bear to leave.

I'm in love with Z., sensed only as a formless, though fervent, affection, since the word lesbian will not enter my vocabulary or consciousness for another two years.

We met soon after my arrival at UMass, when I stomped into her dorm room one night to ask if she could please turn down the music since some of us were studying.

Z. looked away from her friends, took a slow toke of her joint and

asked, "Do you think the weight in The Band's song is a spiritual or a social one?"

A bewildering question. "What band?"

She jacked her thumb at the stereo where "The Weight" was blaring, "*The* Band. God, where do you hang out?"

"The library."

She leaned over and yanked a yearbook from the depths of a large mound and fanned the pages looking for . . . there . . . she handed it to me, pointing to a picture of the basketball team in motion. "My boyfriend. What do you think?" He was black.

"He's tall," I said.

She laughed, held out the joint and made room for me on the bed.

In a time and place when, for most women, college was what you did until you got married and graduate school was the consolation prize for not snagging a man, Z., fueled by an inner drive disconnected from the social norm of femininity, was bold and iconoclastic. She thought for the pure pleasure of stretching her brain, wore clothes for comfort not fashion, and introduced me to the world of pop culture, replacing my repertoire of *Mantovani's 101 Strings* and *Reader's Digest Condensed Books* with whatever taste I would have of drugs and rock and roll. She was my finishing school. Delicately boned, she stood only 5′3″ and weighed barely ninety pounds. I, two inches shorter, felt enormous next to her.

In our senior year, Z. and I were selected to co-teach a discussion section for the Psych 101 class, the only undergraduates to be so honored. Fired up by the tumultuous world flaring around us, we choose our topic: The Sex Role.

We dig for biological data in old college textbooks, argue endlessly for nurture over nature, collect every political broadside we can get our hands on, and bond: emotionally passionate, physically chaste. At weekly TA meetings, Z., ever the bad girl, hammers the graduate student TAs for their antiseptic, clinical approach to teaching. "What the fuck do you *really* care about?" she screams. They're too intimidated to respond, while I, forever the good girl, silently idolize her boldness. I am in love.

Z. invades my dreamworld with vivid, sexual deliciousness: strokes my stomach, grazes my neck, sucks my lips. The morning after, I innocently, joyfully tell her my dream. To her credit she doesn't bolt. But neither is she interested in me, in that way. Instead, she's in love with a charismatic and arrogant boy who treats her cruelly. He demands, she acquiesces; he pushes, she tumbles. I watch helplessly, and over Christmas break, visit her in the hospital where she's recovering from a painful miscarriage. "I know better," she says, "but I'm in love." I hold her hand and wonder at the paradox of her feistiness and passivity, her boldness and vulnerability. Perhaps it is this, her contradictions, that so compels me.

Christmas break is over. Z. is out of the hospital. The spring semester has begun. And I'm reading a book. *The Book,* by Alan Watts, is required for my class in world religions. I stretch across my bed in the afternoon light—the dorm is quiet, my roommate is in class—and in the innocent turning of a page my life breaks apart. Why this book and not some other? The words I read are simply black ink marks on paper. Yet the descriptions of the never-ending cycles of life and death, especially death, plug into some inner dark cave of my soul. Demons, dormant for years, growl awake, charged by a dread so physical that I'm convinced thoughts can kill, like the young healthy men of some cultures who mysteriously die of fright in their sleep. Instead, it is just the illusions of the world that have slipped, revealing Death at the core, leaving me trembling.

I lie alert through the night, listening to banal sounds—a toilet flushes, my roommate snores—and think only of death. My death. I'm held frozen by a current of anxiety alternating with terror so overpowering that my circuits overload. I must unplug. If that means annihilation, so be it.

I'm morbidly suicidal. Obsessed with death. Plan my way to its door. I decide first on carbon monoxide, but quickly reject it when I realize it's actually asphyxiation. Suffocation is not a state I can yield to. Then there's pills. It's the late sixties and drugs are plentiful. Downers are traded in the dorm corridors at night. Everyone takes them: to ease coming off speed, to intensify sex. I, of course, smoke pot, though my preference is for uppers, particularly speed, which whips me into a life-affirming frenzy. Other

drugs scare me, especially LSD. I do not want to open the doors of perception. I do not want to see.

I amass bottles of pills: pink ones, yellow ones, white ones and black. But being indecisive, it is the slow female way that gets me first: I stop eating. In a few days the nausea from lack of food makes me so ill I couldn't eat if I wanted to. The simple thought of a pizza, a salad, or potatoes lurches my stomach. The most I can manage is a few nibbles of dry bread. In three weeks I drop twelve pounds, break the hundred pound barrier and am falling.

Death shadows every waking moment. The lack of food weakens me. I sleep. Fourteen hours a day. Fifteen. Sixteen hours, shutting off the sizzling circuits in my mind, shutting out the world. Sleep becomes my drug of choice. I am breaking down, dropping weight, losing my mind. The adults—my teachers, my supervisor at work—pay no attention. I am drywall, blending into the background. I don't stand out. No one notices.

Occasionally I must go home. There is a wedding to plan, after all.

My family pretends all is fine, which is ludicrous since I've become the bitch queen. Surprisingly, no one confronts me. Perhaps they rationalize my sullen bride-to-be behavior as prenuptial jitters. Outright rebellion would be kinder. Instead, ever the good girl, I tread the passive-aggressive way and reject every idea that my excited mother and grandmother lay before me. Why *should* I wear makeup? No, I *don't* like that invitation. I *loathe* that gown. I won't be caught *dead* wearing ruffles. My sister, desperate to ease the tension—the role of family peacemaker has fallen to her—buys a cocktail dress off the rack of a local department store, saving us all the ordeal of visiting bridal shops. I'm getting married for them, not me, on a fast moving train I can't jump off. If this marriage takes place, I know I will die. If it doesn't, I know I'll be punished. A classic double bind of my own making.

I hate these trips home and make as few as possible. I don't want my family to see me this out of control. But only my sister seems aware of my turmoil. She wants to help, but at age eighteen has little experience with which to handle the depth of my confusion and pain. The adults in my family don't seem to notice, except once.

Saturday morning. Soft early light. I sit in Nana's sunny yellow kitchen and push the burnt toast around on my plate. Nana stands at the stove making coffee. She dumps a handful of ground beans into a small saucepan of boiling water and watches it churn for a few minutes. She is in a stew, ranting about one sister or another who slighted her for this or that. She flicks off the flame, strains the muddy liquid into her cup, and comes to the table.

"What's wrong with you?" she asks.

Wild horses can't drag it out of me.

She cools the coffee with her breath, takes a gulp and launches. "When I was in my fifties," she says, "it was a bad time. I woke up screaming in the middle of the night. I thought I was going to die. I was afraid to die. But you know what? I came through it and you will, too. It'll turn out all right." She doesn't press me about what I'm feeling or explain why she's telling me this story. There is no need. I wouldn't have said anything anyway. The shame cuts too deep.

She rises out of her chair and exits, leaving me alone at the kitchen table. Nothing more is ever said.

I can't share my fears with C., who in my mind is part of the problem. He is kind and loving, a softy, ill-prepared for my raging demons. He gently asks what's wrong. I say nothing. A lie. I don't want to hurt him, an excuse to hide my own cowardliness, which only deepens my feelings of worthlessness and guilt. C. holds me while I cry. Z., however, reads my soul.

Many hours are spent with her, talking about death and suicide and what I've dubbed the absurdity of life. Z. listens intently. Appreciates. And, I know, loves me. Unconditionally. "Read Sartre and Camus," she says and inhales a lung full of smoke. "You're having an existential crisis." The label structures what is formless. Through naming, order and safety are bestowed on my world.

Ah. An existential crisis. Maybe I'm not so crazy after all. Then again, maybe I am.

I think back on my childhood and relabel my eight-year-old moment: suicide. Can I do this? Call what I felt at eight suicidal? Here is a word I didn't use then. At eight I described it this way: I want to run in front of a car. I want to drink poison. I want to die. It is only now at twenty-one, experiencing a rerun of my childhood despair, that I rewrite that feeling as suicidal. I bring order and social meaning to a messy desire that defies simple categorizing. This changes everything: I have a pattern of behavior, a psychological flaw, a burden to carry through life.

My eight-year-old experience is redefined as a nervous breakdown, which is how, with my new education and reading, I also label this premarriage moment. Nervous breakdown means nuts. Crazy. Suicide is wrong. Sick. It marks me as mentally ill. In this moment of language, I progress from being a child in pain to being a young woman with a fixable problem. I move from the soul to medicalization. It is at this moment that I see my first shrink.

I turn up at the student health center and am assigned the first available appointment with the first available psychiatrist.

I walk into the psychiatrist's office. He is bald. He wears a bow tie and sits on his couch in his shirtsleeves thumbing through my file, licking the tip of his index finger to better turn the page. I explain my problem: I'm overwhelmed with thoughts of death and the only way to end the pain is to kill myself. "How?" he asks. I confess the bottles of pills. Tears. He hands me a tissue. Scans my file again. Tells me this wish for death is silly. You have good grades. You've been accepted to a top-notch graduate school. You have a wonderful fiancé you're about to marry. "I don't understand the problem," he says. I loathe this man, walk out of his office, and never come back.

And then there is H., the psychology professor for whom Z. and I teach our discussion section. He smokes pot and invites the best students, me included, over to his house for dinners. Big pots of spaghetti sauce simmer on the stove all day, so acidic that my stomach churns during the long evenings of intense political argument—racism, sexism, the war in Vietnam, the war at home—and loud rock and roll. H. is thirty: old enough to look up to, but young enough to believe. I feel grown-up and like him more than a little.

One day after class, H. hunts me down to ask if I'm okay. A shrug suggests, maybe, and then again, maybe not. It's a test. He has to guess. And he passes by ordering me to come by his office that night to talk.

I approach our meeting with anticipation and fear.

I slouch in the orange plastic chair beside his gray metal desk. The window behind him is pitch black with night. He looks me in the eye and simply asks, "What's wrong?"

Pain, death, dread, guilt, eight years old, fear, humiliation, terror, marriage pour out of me in an incoherent narrative whose meaning is clear. The mention of suicide angers him. He asks me if I've thought how.

I nod. Pills.

Hardness edges his voice. "If you really want to die, I'll help you. But why trust pills? And there are faster ways then starving yourself to death. If you're that serious, I'll push you out the window." He grabs my shoulders and with a vicelike grip drags me to the window. The ground is far enough below to make his threat real. His directness is a cold shock of ice.

I break into loud, gulping sobs. His arms enfold me. We sink to the floor and he rocks me back and forth, back and forth, as a father would comfort a child. He holds my gaze, my pain. With him on guard, I can let go, he will mind the store. My armor splits open and my heart flows to the comfort of his body. There is no longer Michelle, no longer H., huddled on the floor of this cold, sterile office, only a strange fleshy creature: skin, muscles, hair, elbows, and knees, rocking, rocking. The merger of two souls. Intimacy without sex. Compassion. Grace. Across the emotional bridge that binds us pours empathy and a bodiless love. And instead of drowning, I rise with the feeling, up from the depths of the pit and as we burst through the surface of darkness, the light blazes. "Hope is the thing with feathers / That perches in the soul / And sings the tune without the words / And never stops at all."[1]

This mystical moment will haunt me for years. I will long to reexperience it, to duplicate its intimacy, but I will be unable to reach it for

recurrent terminology

decades. For now, however, my demon's death grip is broken. Still, I lack the courage to follow my heart. I can't step off the marriage train careening through my life.

One night Z. asks, "Why are you getting married? I mean *really*." And I tell her about my dream . . .

The telephone rings and I answer it. Nana is on the other end and says "Hello," which surprises me at first since in my dream she is already dead. She is talking to me from beyond the grave. She tells me that she knows I don't want to marry, but I must. She tells me I will be the only grandchild she will ever see married and that I owe her this. She tells me I must marry for her, before she dies. I hang up the phone knowing I have no choice.

That June, a week before graduation, C. and I marry.

There is little I remember about the wedding, in part because I couldn't see. My mother, insisting a bride shouldn't wear glasses, plucked mine from my head as I was about to walk down the aisle. Whatever was experienced on that night I so dreaded is blurred by severe myopia, physical and psychological.

After the wedding, C. and I check into a local motel for our first night of state-sanctioned sex. I worry that someone will break into the room. All night I glance over to the door, checking and rechecking to make sure the chain is still engaged. It is. But anyone could easily kick through it. At one point, while C. is in the bathroom, I tiptoe over to it and run my hand across its cold metal skin. Reassuring. But only for a moment.

Two months after my wedding Nana died from a massive heart attack. I was, in fact, the only grandchild she was to see married. In her final moments, the doctors cut open her chest in a heroic attempt to massage her heart back to life. Defeated by death, they left Grampy in the room with her. He gathered her bloody body up in his arms and kissed her farewell.

Three years later my grandfather died and I flew home to his funeral, an experience that can't be retrieved from memory. I do, however, remember a conversation with my sister in the days following his death. She told me that in the last year of his life Grampy dated two widows, spending alternate weekends with each one. After his death they discovered each other, for the first time, and comparing notes they realized he had asked each for her hand in marriage.

It is now 1997 and I watch a home movie of my twenty-first year. It is the only reel of film with me, and not my father, behind the camera. It's poorly shot: much of it is out of focus, overexposed, handheld, and jumpy.

The film shows a group of college kids gathered in the woods of western Massachusetts: long-haired boys wearing T-shirts and raggedy army fatigues, girls wearing tight jerseys and bell-bottom jeans, their long straight hair blowing in the wind. These are my friends—Z., Marlene, Brian, and C.—from whom I was inseparable during my final college year. It's spring and we play in the woods—catching the rays, fording a shallow stream, flying a kite—for what will be our last time together before my wedding and our graduation.

There is also Red, who has just returned from Vietnam. It is 1970. The war is still raging, campuses exploding. I'm about to move to Madison, Wisconsin, where I will discover politics and Marxism, will taste my first tear gas, and will hear a building blow up. Red has come home from the war hooked on smack. But since we've all dropped acid, taken speed, smoked pot, or popped downers, his drug seems exotic, but not dangerous. Of course, none of this is inscribed on the images.

Z. stands behind a spring-wound Bolex shooting her final project for the film course she's taking. This project is our excuse for being in the woods. Marlene chain-smokes, Red tortures frogs fished from a nearby pond, and in one shot, Z., now behind my father's home-movie camera, captures C. and me in a lovey-dovey kiss. Brian turns somersaults I film in slow motion. Life seems joyful. My suicidal moment has passed, leaving me gaunt but hopeful. I'm about to go off to graduate school to become a psychologist, studying the mysteries of the brain. My marriage will unravel within three years and I will reinvent myself once again, this time as a woman who is smart, independent, a lover of women, and middle class.

I accept the fact that I'm susceptible to suicidal depressions, a burden

to carry for the rest of my life. It makes me afraid to feel life too deeply. I live at the emotional mean, avoiding the lows and, sadly, the highs. It's the peace I make with myself since the idea of ever falling into the black pit again is intolerable.

The story is . . . I'm crazy. *what is the truth?*

The Story in 1956 . . .

The table is set. A soft-boiled egg. A plate of butter. A glass of milk. Two pieces of toast. A small sugar bowl. Nana crosses to the stove and lifts the dented saucepan from the burner. She pours the brown, boiling liquid through a strainer into her coffee cup and reaches for the sugar.

"Oh, let me, let me," I scream, and scoop a spoonful of sugar from the bowl and dive-bomb it into the coffee, watching the little bubbles rise to the surface, foaming a moment before they break. Nana stirs the coffee and takes a sip.

"Mmmm."

"Can I have a taste?" I ask.

"Are you old enough?" I nod, yes, with adult seriousness. "Well, I'm not sure," she teases me.

"Please, oh, please." It's a game we play.

Nana winks. "Okay. But only one taste." She dips the teaspoon into her cup and airlifts it across the table, stalling before my open mouth. "Now don't tell your mother." I vigorously shake my head. "Or Grampy?" I shake my head harder. "It'll be our secret. Promise?"

"I promise," I say, and lap up the sweet coffee with my tongue.

I am eight years old.

We lived in an apartment building in an old suburb of Boston, brick blocks that had seen better days but were not yet crumbling, halfway between the inner immigrant city itself and the leafy, green promise of more prosperous suburbs. Inside our apartment my mother sewed look-alike, frilly-girl dresses for my sister and me in the room where a maid once slept in another time, another class. Outside our apartment my father took home movies of his girls as we paraded our handmade finery up and down the sidewalk for the world to notice.

We lived on the first floor; my grandparents lived on the second floor of the next entryway on the apartment block. Each morning I would peer out the forgotten maid's small bathroom window and look up across the airway to Nana's. She raises her shade, signaling that she's awake, and I run through our back porch, climb out a small opening in the far wall, and up the back flight of stairs. Expecting me, she has opened her back door. I burst into her apartment and arms. She gives me a big kiss, then asks if I've had breakfast yet. I always say no.

The backstairs were a passage, used by no one but us, that linked the two apartments in both space and secrets. This was convenient for everyone. It allowed my sister and me, PJ'd and ready for bed, to run upstairs and kiss Nana and Grampy goodnight. It allowed my grandparents to check in on us when my mother and father went out to dinner with friends. It allowed my grandfather to slip down when he so desired.

My grandfather was raping me. He literally collided with my body and impacted my life—impact, the noun, a violent contact—though I don't remember him ever exerting undue physical force. I wasn't slapped or punched, nor do I remember ever being tied up like my mother was by her brother. My grandfather, I'm sure, believed he was gentle. But the experience carried an emotional impact that felt violent, an abusive and unjust expression of power that cowed me. But, of course, it's not that simple. For there were times when I secretly liked the impact, his attention that made me so special. I, too, had power. The power to attract my grandfather, so pathetic in his need. The power that swelled from his knowing that I *could* spill the secret, even if *I* knew I was too scared to do so.

Grampy puts his thing in my mouth, but I tell no one.

The story was lodged inside me: impact, the verb, meaning "to press into something, pack in." Impaction occurs when something is lodged in a body passage or cavity. It was my grandfather's actions that were lodged in my body. It was his sexual use of me that is the story I can't tell. There is blockage. No movement. It is making me sick.

Middle-of-the-night kid scared. Terror. Creeps into my brain and eats through my body. Devouring me. My heart thumpa thumps. I scream out in pain. Mommy gathers me up in her arms and rocks me.

"What's wrong?" she asks. I am struck mute. Embarrassed. Shamed. I will Mommy to know. She must know. She knows everything. She is my mother. Rock. Rock. Rock. "What's wrong?" *What's wrong?*"

I touch Mommy's panic. She doesn't know. This thought hits my stomach and the universe spins. I hate her. She can never help me. She is not strong enough. Knowing enough. From that moment, that very moment, I know I am on my own. I must help myself. And I do. I do.

I vacate my body, pick up my brain, and let it pull me into the future. This act is so complete, so final, that I forget the pieces I leave behind.

My favorite bedtime story is *The Three Sillies*, which my father reads to us every night, the pages falling naturally open to the spot, bookmarked by brown stains and smudged fingerprints.

Once upon a time, a worldly young man fell deeply in love with a beautiful young woman. They wanted to marry and so, following the custom of the day, she took him home to dinner to meet her parents. The food was tasty and the talk was long, so long in fact, that their tongues went dry and they were thirsty.

The mother, being a good hostess, went down to the cellar to draw some beer. The family waited and waited, but she never returned. Worried, the father went off to find her. And he, too, disappeared. The bride-to-be and her beau stared at each other across the table. "Let me see what's keeping them," she said, smiling to keep up appearances. And she, too, disappeared down into the cellar.

The suitor was left alone at the table. Curious, he went searching. He found the family huddled together at the bottom of the basement stairs crying, the tap to the barrel open, the beer flowing freely onto the floor. The suitor turned off the tap. Then he said, "Why are you three crying and letting the ale wash down to the floor?"

The young woman pointed to an ax stuck in the wooden beam above their heads. "Suppose we got married," she said, "and we had a son. And our son grew up. And one day he came down to the cellar to draw some beer. And suppose on that fateful day the ax fell and killed him. What a dreadful thing it would be." And the father and mother wailed.

Disgusted, the suitor simply reached up, plucked the ax from the beam and lay it disarmed at their feet. He said, "I will leave and not return unless I find three people sillier than you." And, of course, he did.

The first silly was actually an entire village of sillies trying to rescue the moon's reflection—which they mistook for the real thing—from a pond with their rakes and shovels. The second silly was an old farm woman pushing her cow up a steep ladder to feed off the hay on her cottage's thatched roof. The third silly was a companion at the inn, who awakened our hero by running across the room and trying to leap into his trousers, which were hung from the doorknob.

The suitor had found three sillies sillier than the family of his betrothed. He returned and married the beautiful young, though silly, woman. "And if they didn't live happily ever after, that's nothing to do with you or me."[1]

This story entranced me with its suggestion of a permanent, uneasy bargain between the man and the girl, the rational and the silly, the mind and the body. I, of course, identified with the hero, who settled for the ambiguous compromise. This fairy tale, without a simpleton's happy ending, was in step with the world that surrounded me, my home.

I demanded this story night after night, its repeated telling becoming a prayer, the blueprint for a life. By the halfway mark of my childhood, I had memorized its intent—the practical over the fanciful, mind over mindlessness—by putting my trust in the intellect and avoiding silliness and all other emotions associated with the body. I believed in the power of the mind, above all else, and the truth of a permanent, uneasy bargain between it and the body.

Screaming in the middle of the night, my body clutched in a dark pit of pain, I think: My thoughts are making my body sick.

Symptoms bloomed. I avoided bathrooms. They held an unnamed terror.

I wait by the school for Mommy. She's supposed to pick me and my friends up after Brownies. The rest of the children have gone home long ago. An empty cement and treeless school yard. An ancient brick building.

Joanie and Peggy gossip about boys and who's cuter, Bobby or Ira. Miss Bryant moved Ira in front of Joanie today.

"Maybe he'll kiss you," says Peggy.

"Shut up," says Joanie.

I lean against the big green door, ignored. They think me, Shelly, a klutz. I have to pee. Bad. I glance up the street hoping to see Mommy's car coming over the hill. The time ticks away. I have to go to the bathroom. I can't go to the bathroom. Mommy will be here any second. The insistent itch of needing to pee blossoms into stomach-clutching cramps. I wiggle against the door, like a cat rubbing against a post, trying to distract myself. Joanie catches me.

"Ants in your pants?"

I turn bright scarlet and waddle into the building, legs squeezed together, head hanging down.

The inside is black after the bright outdoors. I run down the stairs, sucking in short breaths so as not to disturb my tummy. At the bottom I freeze. Alert. The long narrow basement tunnel stretches out before me — gray concrete floor, rough whitewashed walls, heating pipes bolted overhead, naked bulbs dangling from long wires — a dimly lit, ghoulish basement that strikes me with terror.

At the end of the tunnel lies the bathroom, its etched glass beckoning with its soft glow. I walk toward it, glancing over my shoulder. Too scared to either walk or run, I kind of trot. I reach the bathroom door. Listen for danger. Silence. Push it open.

I take the closest stall and tug at my underpants. My fingers catch in the fabric. Struggling, I somehow manage to pull them off and sit down. I don't lock the stall. A quicker escape. A muffled sound off in the distance. A lock clicks. Footsteps. My head jerks toward the door. I listen intently. Fear washes over me. Silence. I search the silence, unable to move, to pee, to breathe. Silence. In slow motion I rise from the seat and pull up my underpants. I peek out of the stall into the bathroom. It's empty. I tiptoe to the bathroom door and slowly, soundlessly crack it open. The corridor is empty. Silent. I tiptoe out.

I rush up the stairs and back outside, taking my place against the door. Joanie and Peggy have moved on to potato chips, and which are crunchier, Wise or Vitners. I rub my backside against the door, if I can just keep moving. I close my eyes, concentrating on holding it in. A sudden laugh. Warmth between my legs. I look down. A puddle of urine pools on the ground between my feet.

The next day I stay home from school, pretend-sick. I can't go back and face the others.

In fact, I was sick. Sometime during that year, holding on for dear life, I refused to let go of anything: my secret, my own feces. Pains in my stomach, pains in my head, pain everywhere. The doctor, unable to find an organic cause for what ailed me, sent me to the hospital for tests: EEG, EKG, upper GI, lower GI, X-rays, and other tests I no longer remember. All were negative. I'm admitted to the hospital.

The Boston Floating Children's Hospital is another very old building. Long narrow corridors broken by brown doors with heads of clouded glass. Ochre-glazed bricks crawling up giant walls. Tall-ceilinged, closetlike rooms. A space out of proportion to a child's small body, its cavernous size both safe and strange, mostly safe because it is so foreign. I ask about the name and am told that the hospital used to be on a ship, floating in the harbor. In my imagination it still is. I climb the stairs, walk through the doorway, and enter a world that floats away from home and family.

If the incest was the defining experience of my childhood, my illness was its only marker, and the hospital my escape from home and the abuse it sheltered. The hospital announced: safety here. I would spend much of my adolescence and adult years trying to rediscover that place. It is not until age thirty-nine when asthma sends me back into a hospital that I find that place again and can grasp a doctor's coat in my fist and blurt out the secret I've waited over thirty years to speak. "He puts his thing in my mouth," I say, in that gleaming teaching hospital—rooms glass-walled for easy observation and little privacy, cinder-block corridors dressed up with the happy primary colors of children, a place of heroics and action and do everything imaginable but do no harm—and in speaking come full circle.

"Are you Jewish?" I ask everyone I meet: Visiting family members. Sick children. Doctors. Nurses. Anyone who crosses my path. I'm desperate not to be the only one. Only one what? Jew? Child putting her mouth around her Grampy's thing? One day I ask the lady who runs the recreation room where we kids play. She looks up from the book she's reading to a small circle of children, smiles, and says, "Yes." A tight fist in my body relaxes. I have found another Jew. (Stand-in for an abused child? A question I can't utter?) I am not alone in this huge, strange world.

I dread the coming of one o'clock. Visiting hours. Nana and Mommy. They come with hugs and kisses and I sneak peeks at the clock that hangs on the wall, watching its big hand jump out the minutes. When the clock strikes four I announce visiting hours are over. They have to go. Now. They leave.

I skip down the corridors, ducking into each room and checking on how each new friend is doing.

This was the fifties. Children's hospitals were populated with polio victims trapped in wheelchairs and iron lungs. Children who couldn't walk. Children who couldn't breathe. Mobile, I was powerful. In this land of paralyzed, truly infirm children, I was special.

Every morning I visit my friends. I sit in a chair at the head of Jimmie's iron lung and talk to him through the mirror angled over his face. Sometimes he asks me to read him a story because he doesn't have hands to hold the book; they're trapped inside the shiny metal shell that my eyes glue to. And there's Jill, an older girl. I push her along the corridor, feeling grown-up and important. I place pearly red and yellow perfume balls in her clawed hand and twirl them around so she can inspect their perfect roundness. Sometimes, when no one is looking, I steal a wheelchair and fly down long, echoing hallways. It's much faster than walking, more fun, too. Sometimes I race the hallways with the other kids, but they always win, having more practice.

These children fascinated me. If the thoughts in my head were making me sick, I wondered if the same were true for them. And if my thoughts of death were giving me pain, I couldn't imagine what thoughts they could have, big enough to paralyze.

childlike thoughts

The doctors finally diagnosed fecal impaction. I had stopped eliminating. They could find no organic cause, no tumor, no blockage. And I was not telling. I got enemas twice a day. Feces. Dirty. Filthy lucre. My parents were having angry fights about money. My grandmother was in the midst of her twenty-year affair. Her lover gave her, us, things that money could buy: vacations, steaks, clothes, Havana cigars. Things we couldn't otherwise afford.

Grampy smokes smelly cigars. He has a bulbous nose and thick lips. He clears his throat and coughs up thick globs of phlegm with a loud growl. And always a cigarette hangs from his lips. The ash on the tip grows longer and longer until it drops onto his stomach. "Oh Ben," whines Nana, "can't you watch what you're doing?" All his shirts have small burn holes down the front. He smells. Of cigars and cigarette smoke. Of the gasoline that he pumps all day. In the gas station he shuffles out to a waiting car. Cranks the pump. Fills the tank. All the while a lit cigarette hangs from his lips. The ash growing, growing, growing. When will it drop? Before he finishes pumping the gas? Will it fall into the oily puddle of gasoline at his feet? Will he die in a fiery explosion?

My grandfather, in turn, was fucking me.

I reach out to touch it. My fingers hover above the smooth, round top. "Pet it," he whispers. It sways back and forth. "Like a kitty." I hesitate. His fingers close around my wrist. I sniff gasoline. His fingernails are dirty. He bites his nails. Like me. A little flap of skin he forgot to bite off. I almost touch it. My finger is warmed by the heat from his blue skin. What if it burns? I pull my hand back. He holds on tight. My hand moves nowhere. "Pet the kitty, sweetheart. He won't bite." A tiny drop of something smelly oozes out the tip. Yuck. The smell fills my nose. Sweet. My mouth fills with saliva. I can't swallow it. I taste the smell. My mouth fills up with spit. I have to swallow. I can't swallow. I clamp my mouth shut. A bit of wet escapes and dribbles down my chin. I clamp my lips tighter. Warm liquid dribbles down between my legs. Everything is blurred. Tears pop into my eyes. Roll down my face. Everywhere is wet. Wet.

The wall descends. All is blank.

There is no story . . .

The Story in 1997 . . .

This is a story about love. Of a grandmother who loved too tight, of a grandfather whose love was corrupted, of an artist's love for her art, and of the love of one woman for another.

Five years after Q. and I separated, we came back together. My mother and father, upon hearing the news, laughed and said they weren't surprised, that we had the strangest divorce they'd ever seen. During our separation, Q. bought a house around the corner from our house, which I now owned. We talked constantly, dropped in for daily visits, and turned to each other first to ponder self-discoveries learned in the new and separate lives we had each built. There was between us the pull of history seasoned by mutual respect and an enduring emotional attachment.

During the separation, a time of solitude alternating with other relationships—her women, my (mostly) men—I finally embraced my dependency on others, while Q. learned that she thrived on her own. We both inched toward some golden mean of relating, traveling toward each other to a place where we gave more than we took, and saw the other more for who they were than for what we desired. This second phase of our life together seems different from our first thirteen years; we are less often snarled by the web of old patterns or cut on the sharp shards of our childhoods. There is, between us, contentment and joy.

This also is a story of my love of film. Of images that spoke in the absence of words, and celluloid that storehoused feelings as long as the emotions surrounding the incest—terror, sexual excitement, shame—contaminated all feelings. Unable to penetrate the wall of amnesia, I constructed images from the elements of my craft—actors, spaces, and light—and projected them onto a wall, *the* wall, to hint at what it obscured. And slowly the beam of light burned peepholes through that wall, revealing some of what lurked behind it, although I sometimes suspect that the secrets were merely the motivation, while the films, themselves, the real thing revealed.

Mine is not the story of a bad life, but rather the search for an understanding of the three moments of collapse in an otherwise thriving one. These episodes of madness, what William Styron describes in his book *Darkness Visible* as "despair beyond despair," were actually bouts of extreme depression, a consequence of the sexual abuse I experienced so young. Without the incest, I believe I never would have experienced the "hopelessness that crushes the soul."

My life has been marked with loving relationships, many close friends, and gratifying work, as filmmaker and as teacher, that feeds both heart and mind. Paradoxically, the ability to compartmentalize allowed me a productive and contented life. By banishing the bad I could experience the good, circumscribed perhaps, but also decontaminated. My driving need to control, ironically, reinforced a belief that I could have an impact on my life and the world, giving me a continuing sense of agency, optimism and hope.

There are many stories that remain hidden here.

There is my sister, who brought an intimacy to my childhood not charged with danger. We were each other's best friends and confidants, two little girls who anchored each other against the family storm of power and sex that roared about us. Because I was an object of the abuse, I believed she was protected from it, which gave my hurt purpose and my childhood meaning. Though we shared the same childhood space, we experienced it differently, each from our own point of view. A gifted musician and teacher, she has her own story to tell.

There is also my father, a good and kind man, who seldom appears on these pages, appropriately since he was eclipsed by my mother's family. He bought me my first Erector set and my first microscope, opening the path of my escape, my mind. He also gave me the shoeboxes filled with family home movies, images that he shot with an unschooled talent.

The home movies. When I watch them, pieces of the past float back to

me. Or I think they do. In fact, there are moments when I can't be sure if a memory is an accurate image of my lived experience or an illusion of a memory anchored in the movie images themselves. Do I really remember twirling my baton? Electric blue satin drum-majorette dress against soft red walls. My mother watching lovingly, my father, proudly, behind the camera. Or do I just think I remember because repeated viewings of the home movies have imprinted these scenes on my mind?

I have spent the last forty years of my life struggling to unlock the secrets of the past. Self-understanding is a strong yet elusive desire because the line between self-knowing and self-deception is as thin as time itself. There are many things I will never know. What it's like to be my mother, how Q. experienced our relationship, how my childhood memories are filtered through adult experiences. How do I know that what I write here is actually what I experienced and not memory skewed by what was learned in the intervening years? In part, I'm helped by journals kept since I was eleven years old. In part, my art has shaped the shadows, creating narratives of my childhood refined over time. With these guides I have formed my necessary fictions: fictions in that their truthfulness to the events of my life can't always be definitively known; necessary in that their creation spins the web of narrative through which life moves. These are not lies I tell myself, but truths that can only find expression through fiction. Necessary Fictions. Revealing Fictions. Living Fictions. Each hints at a different nuance of meaning. All are appropriate, none are adequate.

new, different perspectives

Necessary fictions serve the truth even if they can't definitively pin down the truth. Often they can only be judged by the devious clue: the wound that heals, the pain that eases, the art that grows, the symptom that resolves, and the relationship that, no longer suffocated, begins to breathe. Their goal is self-knowledge not self-deception, integrity not self-flattery or, alternatively, self-flagellation. They are at odds with dishonest fiction, which serves ends other than the truth: revenge for pain suffered, humiliation for a betrayal endured. Necessary fictions ride on the moral and ethical undercurrents that flow through all our lives. As Ian Hacking has written,

We constitute our souls by making up our lives, that is, by weaving stories about our past, by what we call memories. The tales we tell of ourselves and to ourselves are not a matter of recording what we have done and how we have felt. They must mesh with the rest of the world and with other people's stories, at least in the externals, but their real role is in the creation of a life, a character, a self.[1]

I approach my necessary fictions with adventure and a sane pinch of both skepticism and fear. After all, further fictions may not fall into line. Necessary fictions require a willingness to not know, while at the same time, enough conviction to commit to a plausible narrative deduced, with honesty, from the evidence at hand. Their ambiguity, their uncertainty, should always be honored.

The story is . . .

Art

Art is a lie that makes us realize truth, at least the truth that is given us to understand.
::   Pablo Picasso

Daughter Rite

A Film by Michelle Citron

NOTE: *This film alternates between two visual styles: home movies and documentary film. The home movies, all from the fifties, are of my family. They were shot by my father and show a mother and her two young daughters—my mother, my sister, and me—doing activities familiar to anyone who has taken home movies. These images, however, are manipulated: motions are repeated and slowed down revealing that which is hidden from the eye at normal speed. Through this technique the home movies reveal the subtle, nonverbal communication that occurs within families. The documentary footage of Stephanie and Maggie is shot with the roving, exploring camera of cinema verité documentary. These scenes are "fake." They are, in fact, fiction: scripted, directed, and acted. In Daughter Rite, the authentic documentary images—the home movies—are manipulated to look like experimental film. On the other hand, what looks like real documentary is actually a fiction. The film confounds audience's expectations: seeing is not believing. The overall style of the film asks the question: "Is there a difference between narrative fiction truth and documentary truth?"*

FADE UP: **for Sue and Vicki**

1. Home Movie: School Picnic   DAY/EXT.

Colors—red, black, yellow—move in slow motion across the screen. Gradually the image becomes readable: A Mother and her young Daughter, age ten, walk back and forth across a field full of people. They are participants in an old-fashioned contest. Each holds the handle of a spoon

in her mouth. At the end of one spoon is an egg, which they pass carefully between them as they walk.

NARRATOR: (Over the home-movie images) I started this film when I was twenty-eight. My twenty-eighth birthday was particularly difficult for me. For months before I was depressed, waking up anxious almost every morning at 5 A.M., having trouble falling asleep at night, losing weight. I had trouble working, concentrating, focusing my attention. Twenty-eight was so old, so final. Just before my birthday I suddenly remembered that in my mother's twenty-eighth year she had married and then had her first child—me. And here I was entering into my twenty-eighth year, and I was not married or having a child. Turning twenty-eight and not doing like my mother, I realized I was very scared. And it was this fear on my twenty-eighth birthday that started the process which has become this film. I am now thirty. I dedicate this film with love, to my mother, a woman who I am very much like and not like at all.

FADE OUT

TITLE FADES UP: **Daughter Rite**

2. Home Movie: Public Gardens, Boston   DAY/EXT.

A pedal-driven Swan Boat filled with tourists. On the boat sit the Mother and her two Daughters. They wave at the camera as the boat glides by.

NARRATOR: (Over the home-movie images) The phone call was from Mom. She sounded very depressed. Dad had just moved out. She was angry because Dad took the bedroom set, which they had agreed would be hers. But she doesn't need it, she already has one. Obviously she was upset and it took the form of this complaint. Then she told me she had changed her mind again, she'd put the house back on the market and she was moving to Hawaii. I told her I thought the idea was irrational, especially since she herself had gone there to check it out and had admitted it was foolish and impractical to move there. I told her it was just a reaction to Dad moving out, being alone and having reality hit. I was so upset—not by the divorce, but by her moving to Hawaii. She's so dishonest with herself. Snap, snap, change the environment and everything will be better. Living out a fantasy. In Paradise, everyone is happy. The superficial and desperate change. She will still be the same person there, unhappy with herself, her life, running away. Why is she so scared? Her reaction to Dad, her inflexibility, tell me she's been wanting to leave for a long time, it is just that now she's been wronged, she has the excuse to leave.

The family gets off the boat and walks toward the camera. The Mother has her arm around the Youngest Daughter, the Older Daughter waves to the camera.

NARRATOR: This way she doesn't have to take responsibility for leaving. It was his fault. Why did she need to wait for the excuse? Why couldn't she leave before? I hate her dishonesty.

FADE OUT

FADE IN:

3. Kitchen. Mother's House   DAY/INT.

STEPHANIE *and* MAGGIE, *two sisters in their late twenties, sit at a table in the sunny kitchen, drinking coffee and talking directly to the camera. Dark-haired* MAGGIE *is the older sister; blond-haired* STEPHANIE *is the younger.*

STEPHANIE: Well, I was in labor for twenty-three hours, until they finally took Anna cesarean. My mother had flown in to be with me after the birthing of the child and all that. Well, at the hospital, she and Steven were there and I was in a labor room, and they only allowed one person in at a time. And after about ten hours into it, I got very tired and I was in a lot of pain too, screaming just like all the movies, really. And I found that when she was in there that I hurt more, that I was more tired. Do you know what she would do? She would hold my hand and she would say, "It's all right, honey, it's all right." Honey, honey! Like I had a bad tummy ache or something, and it would go away. I was so mad. Finally, when Steven came in about the tenth and a half hour or something, I said, "I don't want her in here anymore." Yeah, because Steven was giving me the strength that was a lot easier to handle, it was like he knew that I would be all right, he knew that I had the strength to do it. And so he said, "She doesn't want you in anymore," and he stayed in with me, up until they brought me into the operating room. And she's never forgiven me for that. Not ever. It's like I denied her right of being a mother, to be there and take care of me. And that's exactly what I did not need at that time.

FADE OUT

FADE IN:

4. Home Movie: The Promenade   DAY/EXT.

 *The Mother and her two Daughters, ages three and six, walk toward then away from the camera, parading for the father behind the lens. Their movement is jerky, unnatural, repetitious.*

NARRATOR: (Over the home-movie images) Mom's moving away. Six thousand miles. And she won't even stop in Madison for a day to visit me before she leaves. She has to get to Hawaii quickly to buy a house. $82,000. Merrily she goes off into debt. One day. What difference would it make to her? If I want to see her I can, for a few hours while she's changing planes in Chicago. A six-hour drive to see her for two hours, and she won't even spend a day with me. I understand, getting divorced, ending everything, breaking all ties. Everyone is giving her such a hard time, being so unsupportive, she probably feels defensive. If she lets up on just one thing, she will never have the power to break loose. Visiting me is that one thing? Oh, fuck her.

Another day. The Mother and Daughters parade their finery for Dad's camera eye. They move away from the camera, over and over, caught in an endless loop.

NARRATOR: (Over the home-movie images) Yesterday I met Mom at the airport for two hours between flights, as she flies off into the western horizon to Hawaii and a new life. Sad and painful. Our time together was good, substantive, not the usual small talk. I felt very close to her. I cried all the way home. I have no more home, no more childhood, no more mother. It is over.

FADE OUT

FADE IN:

5. Home Movie: Washing the Dinner Dishes   NIGHT/INT.

The two young Daughters wash and dry the dishes and hand them, clean, to the Mother for her approval.

NARRATOR: (Over the home-movie images) Mom called yesterday. After talking about the weather and her new job, she said she had something she wanted to talk to me about—what she wanted when she dies. She wants to have her organs donated to a hospital and then to be cremated. She said she wanted to tell me even though she knew I never liked to talk about such personal things. Her words were all right, but her sarcastic tone implied that I was a closed, secretive, unfeeling, and uncaring person, which is why I wouldn't want to hear what she had to tell me and why she found it difficult to talk to me. Nancy told me, of course Mom feels I'm incapable of love, that is, loving her, because her idea of love is the total sacrificial act. My mother did it for her mother and in turn expects it from us. I am unwilling to see that as love, so I don't offer it. She is unwilling to see anything else as love, so she doesn't accept what I do offer. But the whole interaction unnerved me. I thought, how sad. How little she knows me. And I really felt the loss of never having been close with her, and the loss because we would never be close. Then I got confused, because I always thought I was a feeling, loving person and here was my mother telling me that I wasn't. And I believed her because she was my mother, and she would know me if anyone did.

FADE OUT

FADE IN:

6. Living Room. Mother's House   DAY/INT.

STEPHANIE *and* MAGGIE *sit close to each other on the couch. They look directly into the camera, which pans between them as they speak.*

STEPHANIE: I was very jealous of what she was like with my friends. I was jealous of my friends' relationships with her, and of her relationships with my friends. I didn't have as good a relationship with either my friends or Mother. And you . . .

MAGGIE: Stephanie's relationship with Mother was better than mine.

STEPHANIE: We got along until I was fifteen. And at that time we sort of broke up.

MAGGIE: But, well, Mother demanded a great deal of my life. She wanted to know everything that I was doing. She was very involved in buying me clothes and dressing me, sending me off to parties, and living through me. She didn't have much else at this point. And the more she pushed me, and the more she tried to get from me, the more I pulled back and away from her. And it was hard for her to live with that. I discovered later she was reading my diaries, so I started to hide my diaries and she was also reading my mail. And even after I hid my diaries, I still found out that she was reading them, and then it made me even more angry because she wasn't just happening upon it and reading it because it was there. She was looking for it. It was more an invasion because it was conscious.

STEPHANIE: And, you really, I remember that you just pulled away from her so much. You would go in your room and just shut the door . . .

MAGGIE: . . . which made her so mad. She would tell me, "Will you open that door—we have open doors in this house."

STEPHANIE: Yes—"We are all one family"—right? "And we should know what's going on with each other." And with me it wasn't so bad. She sort of got a lot of that out with Maggie, and so with me, like I brought most of my stuff to her—she didn't have to ask me, she didn't have to read my diary or anything like that. But as we got older, we were, you were very independent of her, and I got more independent of her, and boy . . .

MAGGIE: The thing that was amazing about the letters and the diary is that she felt perfectly justified in doing that. She had no sense of doing something bad to me. She was . . . my mother, and it was her right, it was . . . that was part of her function as mother, making me breakfast in the morning, and reading my mail.

STEPHANIE: And the thing that made her so mad and, like she would tell me this after you went away to school, is that the things that she read in your diary and in the letters just infuriated her because it was just proving that you were not the daughter that she wanted her (*gesturing toward* Maggie) to be. So it was this very cycle thing, where she'd read the diary and she'd get mad at you for who you were, and you would be more like that because you would be so mad at her for doing it . . .

MAGGIE: Going around in circles. That was another reason why she was very good at giving advice to our friends—was because our friends either took the advice, or she thought they took the advice, but all she saw with us was her failures, I . . . we were not the daughters we were supposed to be.

FADE OUT

FADE IN:

7. Home Movie: At Play in the Backyard   DAY/EXT.

Images of the older Daughter swinging on a glider; the Mother smiling for the camera. The images are streaked, as if looking through a curtain of warm reddish and brown tones.

NARRATOR: (Over the home-movie images) Mom just called. She sold her house, a ridiculous fantasy in the first place. But why? I wanted desperately for her to be more practical so she'd be less disappointed. Her life is a series of misjudgments of money and people, always making the wrong choices, always ending up getting screwed. She works so hard to fill up her empty hours. She's selling her car because she can't afford to make the payments and she doesn't go out at night anyway. Alone, lonely, sitting at home. I ask her if she's depressed. She says no, of course not. A lie. There is such a need there, to talk, for both of us. But the patterns of behaving are so thick neither of us ever tears through them. We are both terrified to do so. Talking to her forces an awareness of the helplessness of it all. If only once she would say, "I'm lonely." But then, of course, I live in dread she will actually one day say it. She is so alone, and <u>I have the terrible fear I am just like her and will also grow up to be that isolated and depressed</u>. There is so much pain in her voice I cannot bear the thought that I, too, will one day feel that pain. And of course I do believe that one day I will feel it. Not because everyone feels it, not because her pain is the result of bad choices in an oppressive culture where she had no choice anyway. I fear I'm going to turn out just as lonely as her because I will make all the wrong choices, even worse, since I have no cultural excuse. I present a persona of togetherness and personal power. Yet when I talk to her, I realize her legacy. Deep inside me I don't believe at all in my power or strength.

FADE OUT

FADE IN:

8. Home Movie: Getting Out of the Car

NIGHT/EXT.

EXTREME HIGH ANGLE: *The Mother wears a bright red coat. She gets out of the car and enters the house, oblivious to the camera that watches her from above.*

NARRATOR: (Over the home-movie images) Last night I dreamed. My mother meets a lot of women in a bar on top of a hill. I am there. She is as she was in the late forties—pretty, smiling, lively. She tells us all how wonderful her life is, how she is happy and never lonely. Then she excuses herself to go to the bathroom. A woman comes back to tell me she has locked herself in and is crying. I go to find her. When I arrive, she quickly dries her eyes and nothing is wrong.

FADE OUT

FADE IN:

9. Kitchen. Mother's House

DAY/INT.

STEPHANIE *and* MAGGIE *make a fruit salad.*

STEPHANIE: You know, the first year that I was in college, we had this thing where we would make . . .

MAGGIE *hands* STEPHANIE *a wooden cutting board.*

MAGGIE: . . . You get the crummy one.
STEPHANIE: What's this?
MAGGIE: That's your breadboard.
STEPHANIE: Bleeeeeaaaah!
MAGGIE: I got the pig.

She holds up a cutting board in the shape of a pig.

STEPHANIE: I see the pig.
MAGGIE: I'll cut the apples. Do you want the Macintosh and the Delicious?

MAGGIE *starts chopping; a piece of apple falls to the floor.* STEPHANIE *picks it up.*

STEPHANIE: You'll have to watch out for that.

MAGGIE: I think we're forgetting walnuts.

STEPHANIE *grabs a bunch of bananas off the counter.*

STEPHANIE: Banana! Lots and lots of bananas. A hundred and one tons of bananas!

MAGGIE *pokes at the bananas with her finger, testing their ripeness.*

MAGGIE: Oooh . . .
STEPHANIE: It's on the outside.
MAGGIE: You can feel the mush . . .
STEPHANIE: . . . Yeah, when you're mushing it in like that.
MAGGIE: I wasn't mushing it in.
STEPHANIE: Look at it! Look at this! You're mushing it in!
MAGGIE: You have to feel the texture.
STEPHANIE: I bet you're real hard on cantaloupe and avocados, huh?

MAGGIE *demonstrates her technique on the back of* STEPHANIE's *hand.*

MAGGIE: That's how hard I was mushing. Do you think I was damaging this banana? It could not possibly be damaged more than it is.
STEPHANIE: Listen, that is mostly a good banana.
MAGGIE: Yeah. The top half. Nothing of this bottom half . . .

STEPHANIE *unwraps some very sad-looking celery, brown and slimy.*

STEPHANIE: Well, Mom's had this for a while.
MAGGIE: Oh jeez. Why don't you just throw it away?
STEPHANIE: I don't know, look, there's this whole middle part here.
MAGGIE: God, it spits out at you! You've got to be kidding.
STEPHANIE: Just jumping off the table! Maggie, look at this. No, we'll let this go to heaven, to celery heaven, but, ah, the rest of this is good.

MAGGIE *picks up what is obviously a rotten piece of celery.*

MAGGIE: You're kidding! It's still slimy, it's covered with slime!
STEPHANIE: It's called washing it off.
MAGGIE: Yeah, but it's this funny color, that's all.
STEPHANIE: The middle of celery is always more yellow.

STEPHANIE *starts chopping up the celery for the salad.*

MAGGIE: Are you serious, are you really going to use this?
STEPHANIE: Yes, I'm very serious! You just cut off the bad and use the good. Wash it up, and it's good as new. It is a little brown—

MAGGIE: I wish you wouldn't.

STEPHANIE: I wonder why that gets brown on the inside.

MAGGIE: I don't really like celery in my fruit salad anyway. I like just fruit and nuts.

STEPHANIE: Celery is very good in fruit salad. You come across these little crunchy things, it's real good.

MAGGIE: The fruit is already crunchy.

STEPHANIE: The celery is just fine. Look at this! Look—hard! You know, it's good celery.

MAGGIE: Yeah, but look what it's been sitting in the bag with!

STEPHANIE: Maggie.

MAGGIE: That celery's probably a month old.

STEPHANIE: Maggie. The celery is good. Look at the celery. Look closely at the celery. Look at this—see?

STEPHANIE *takes a bite. It CRUNCHES.*

STEPHANIE: It's crunchy. It's very good celery. We'll just get rid of these . . . bad and uh . . .

MAGGIE: What's the yogurt out for?

STEPHANIE: To put into the salad. What else are you gonna do with it?

MAGGIE: Isn't there any whipped cream in there?

STEPHANIE: You're sitting out here talking about calories and 'biscos and you want whipped cream in your salad? No way!

MAGGIE: A little bit of whipped cream in the salad isn't gonna be bad.

STEPHANIE: There's no whipped cream. Use the yogurt. Yogurt is good for you. Makes you strong.

MAGGIE: Yeah, I just prefer whipped cream.

STEPHANIE: Good for your digestive system. Well, there's no whipped cream.

MAGGIE: All right, I heard you. I see. I have a good idea. Why don't you keep the celery out of the salad until the very end, after I take my portion out, or you can just put celery in your . . . what you want of the salad. I think that's a good idea.

STEPHANIE: You really want me to keep this pile of celery here and not put it into the salad? I mean is that what you really want?

MAGGIE: Yeah, I'd like that.

STEPHANIE: So be it.

MAGGIE: Okay, how much yogurt do we put in here?

MAGGIE *scoops the yogurt out of the container and into the salad bowl.*

STEPHANIE: Hmmmmm . . . that looks . . . that is . . . plenty.

MAGGIE: Well, it's got to coat the fruit, doesn't it?

STEPHANIE: Coat it, yes, but it's not gonna swim in it.

MAGGIE: Looks about ready.

STEPHANIE: Okay, I'll go get my separate bowl. I'll get your bowl, too.

STEPHANIE *gets the bowls from the cupboard and starts serving the fruit salad.*

MAGGIE: Yeah, please. I don't want to eat out of this bowl.

STEPHANIE: Well, I wonder if I should put my celery in before or after.

MAGGIE: After. You want a fork?

STEPHANIE: Yeah.

MAGGIE: That would be a good idea, don't you think?

STEPHANIE: That would be a great idea. Do we have a long fork in there?

MAGGIE: You don't want a baby fork?

STEPHANIE: No, I don't like baby forks. How much celery can I fit into this little bowl?

STEPHANIE *makes a big production of adding the celery pieces to just her bowl.*

STEPHANIE: It's like sprinkles. It's falling out of the bowl. Oh well.

MAGGIE *tastes a spoonful of salad.*

MAGGIE: It would be better with whipped cream. And an orange. I don't really like it. No, I'm not gonna have any.

MAGGIE *pushes her bowl away and reaches for an orange.* STEPHANIE *dumps her serving into the large bowl.*

STEPHANIE: Don't want to waste it.

She then dumps all the celery pieces in and mixes it thoroughly. MAGGIE *eats a slice of orange.*

MAGGIE: Ooh, this is dry.

STEPHANIE *just stares at her, dumbfounded.*

FADE OUT

FADE IN:

10. Home Movie: The Young Daughters at Home NIGHT/INT.

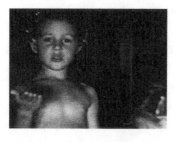

Images of the two young Sisters, dressed in pajamas and curlers, mugging to the camera.

NARRATOR: (Over the home-movie images) Yesterday, putting the old family pictures in the scrapbook. Mom in her early and mid-twenties was beautiful. I look like her. This beautiful woman who is now overweight, with bleached silver hair. I do not want to be like her. Not lonely, not depressed, not prying, not sneaking through the refrigerator when I thought no one was looking, not saying one thing when I mean another. The anger starting, building, festering, year after year. Not having that anger seep out in manipulative ways, not confusing strength and power with control. Not putting others first and then hating them for it. Not being helpless. Not hating my life but being too scared to change it.

FADE OUT

FADE IN:

11. Home Movies: Montage DAY/INT.

The two young Daughters, dressed in their best, walking toward the camera. A shot of a birthday party. The older Sister buckling her younger Sister's shoes. The two Sisters kiss. Walking out of the house, dressed up for a party.

NARRATOR: (Over the home-movie images) Threw a tarot. The Queen of Wands was the outcome. I chose the card as a signifier, meaning my mother. It is my mother. Authority, power, fire like icicles, taming the leopard, which is me, that stands under her hand. The leopard that is also a piece of her power, ready to spring at me on her command. She had a need for control. She would go through my drawers and rearrange them; she would ask to read my mail, peering over my shoulder. She would listen in on my phone calls. I would say no, she would glare, tell me I was selfish to want privacy. To keep to oneself, to hoard was a terrible trait. It meant unloving, selfish; it also meant depriving her of her vicarious life. Shari said I just don't want to admit that card is me, and I would be happier if I did. I see that card as control, and no, I do not want to accept that in me, that which I considered evil in my mother. I hate my weaknesses; my weaknesses are my mother. I hate the dark side of me, my evil, my bitchiness, my selfishness. That part too is my mother. I hate my mother, and in hating my mother, I hate myself.

FADE OUT

FADE IN:

12. Living Room. Mother's House   DAY/INT.

STEPHANIE *and* MAGGIE *sit on the floor, sorting through an old pile of record albums.* STEPHANIE *strokes the cat that sits on her lap.*

STEPHANIE: No, what I can't believe is the amount of records that Mother has.
MAGGIE: Oh yeah.
STEPHANIE: I mean, did you see the pile in her room? And a pile here? And these? She's got Christmas records like this . . .
MAGGIE: Oh yeah . . . Over a hundred Christmas records!
STEPHANIE: I couldn't believe it!
MAGGIE: I remember hearing Christmas records in October. I asked her, you know . . . she spends her money on the weirdest stuff. I can't believe it.
STEPHANIE: And, yeah, she's really broke though. I didn't believe how really broke she was.
MAGGIE: I know.
STEPHANIE: It's really, you know, it scares her. It's really horrible for her to have to think about that right now.
MAGGIE: It makes me mad. I mean, she got money when Dad died. She got that life insurance money . . . I know it wasn't much . . .
STEPHANIE: But that's a long time ago, Maggie . . .
MAGGIE: Yeah, but she had this job for quite a while, and she was also married in the interim. She didn't have to support herself then.
STEPHANIE: Yeah, but she didn't get any money, she hasn't gotten the settlement yet.
MAGGIE: She played such a cute little trick on me today. Such a cute little trick. I went in to see her at the hospital, right? And she didn't say, she didn't ask me for money, but she told me how she just didn't know what

she was going to do about these bills, looked out the window and sighed, and played with the flowers I'd brought her.

STEPHANIE: She asked me.

MAGGIE: For . . . for money?

STEPHANIE: Yeah. She told me that she was really broke and she explained to me what happened, and she asked me if I could give her a loan.

MAGGIE: That's very interesting that she asks you, but she's got to play around with me! She can't come out and ask me.

STEPHANIE: Well, you know . . . Say, Kitty, lay on the albums . . .

STEPHANIE *makes a grab for the cat, who's landed on the albums.*

MAGGIE: Well, what?

STEPHANIE: Well, Maggie, let's face it. You aren't the easiest person to ask for money.

MAGGIE: Well, what do you mean? If you ever needed money, I would always lend it to you.

STEPHANIE: Yeah, I think you would . . . no, no, you would. You would lend it to me. You would. But it would be very hard to ask you for money. I have taken loans before actually asking you because I didn't feel that my reason was valid enough. I didn't want to have to explain myself to the point where I feel like I have to ask you for money. And I'm sure Mother feels even more extreme than that, because you do get so . . . you're very angry at her about that.

MAGGIE: Well, what are . . . what are you going to do with Mother?

STEPHANIE: Well, I'm going to give her the money.

MAGGIE: How much money?

STEPHANIE: Two thousand dollars.

MAGGIE *lets out a long disapproving sigh.*

STEPHANIE: I still belong to the credit union, I can get a loan.

MAGGIE: Two thousand dollars! You are crazy! How can you afford to do that? You are going off to school, you're going back to school, you've just broken up your marriage, you're not getting much money from Steven, you're getting enough to help Anna along.

STEPHANIE: Listen, I've got money for school, that's all set. I can do it. I'll give her the book and she will pay back the loan.

MAGGIE: I bet. I bet she won't. I bet you will wind up borrowing two thousand dollars and have to pay it back all by yourself plus the interest. You . . . God! I don't know.

STEPHANIE: I don't believe that. I don't believe that I'll have to pay it back. I trust her more than that—she isn't going to screw me like that.

MAGGIE: Why not? She screwed me like that!

STEPHANIE: But she hasn't screwed me like that.

MAGGIE: Can't you learn from the experience of others? That's what she did with me . . . that's exactly what she did with me. It wasn't two thousand dollars probably, but . . .

STEPHANIE: It's not the same thing! She reacts to me differently. She hasn't been like that with you for a long time. You just don't have the same experience with her that I do.

MAGGIE: Oh, I think you are crazy.

STEPHANIE: Well, it's just something that I will do. I trust her. I really believe that she will pay me back and it will be . . . I think it will be real good.

MAGGIE: I wish I had that kind of mother. *different relationship for each*

STEPHANIE *shoots her a look.*

MAGGIE: I don't!

STEPHANIE: I wish you did too.

                                                    FADE OUT

FADE IN:

13. Home Movie: Birthday Party Montage   DAY/INT.

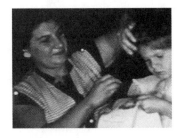

A series of images from various birthday parties. The children are all very young, perhaps two to six years old. They open presents, eat cake and ice cream, blow out candles. The parents are everywhere . . . holding children, helping them eat, handing them gifts, fixing their hair.

NARRATOR: (Over the home-movie images) Last night I dreamed. Nana, Mom, and Nancy are sitting around a round table and they are trying to give me an injection. It is Mom who has the needle, I am their experimental animal. The day before they had given me another injection to see how I would react, and I have gotten very sick. They try to persuade me but I cannot be persuaded. I do not want the injection. They plead, they bargain: "It is for your own good. You'll be doing us an invaluable favor. For the good of mankind. It won't kill you. We wouldn't do anything to hurt you. We love you." I feel victimized and tortured and I do not trust them. Nancy is not doing this. I really sense her supporting me, feeling sorry for me, but she sits passively, neither torturing nor rescuing me. I am very weak and crying and hysterical, but with my last bit of energy I fight them off. I cannot let them give me this injection! A big glass cylindrical thing marked in blue graduated numbers with a long stainless needle filled with a caramel-colored liquid. They keep brandishing it about, holding it upright, squeezing a few drops out at the tip, proving to me they won't inject any air bubbles. At one point they lose all the liquid and have to refill it. They try mainly to verbally coax and cajole. I keep saying "No." And even though they try every form of strong persuasion, they cannot physically force me to take the injection. It is against some rule. Somehow I have to agree to let them do it. The attacks, counterattacks are verbal. I know that all I have to do is bounce their arguments off me. Even though my exhausted body is weakened, I feel that my thinking is clear, meaning that I am not one bit intimidated or confused in my purpose. I might get hysterical, but there is always a little piece of my mind that stays alert and protects me. Clumsily I parry every attack of theirs. I feel them begin to weaken their barrage on me. I begin to feel they are not going to win. Nana offers me some walnuts but I refuse them. I will not be bought off.

FADE OUT

FADE IN:

14. Dining Room. Mother's House   DAY/INT.

Very SLOW ZOOM IN: STEPHANIE *sits at the dining room table telling her story directly into the camera.*

STEPHANIE: When I . . . My mother was gone. She'd gone out to a meeting or gathering of some kind, and I was sitting up in my room and I think I was reading or something like that. And Henry came in . . . he sort of shuffled in and he started . . . he started picking things up on my bureau and putting them down, and moving back and forth and asking me how school was and was I gonna go to the prom. And just ridiculous things that he didn't care about, and he'd never really asked me before. And I knew that something was up. And then he moved from my bureau right toward the bed and he started picking up the bedspread, and picking at it and just saying these things like, "You know, you're really . . . you're really the hottest number in this house." Or . . . I don't even really know . . . remember . . . or like, "I really think you've got something going. It's too bad your mother wasn't more like you . . . I've watched you, I've seen you with the boys." And . . . he lunged for me. And he tore off my clothes. And he raped me. And then he left my room. And when he was leaving, he said, "If you know what's good for you, you're not going to tell your mother about this." And then he left. He left the house. And I sat there for a long time. I don't know how long, all I remember is this . . . I've got this little clock by my bed, and it went tick, tick, tick, tick, tick, tick, tick . . . and I just remember that sound. And finally, like in a daze, I just got up and I took a bath and got my nightgown out. And I was sitting in bed with the covers sort of . . . sort of around me. So tight . . . I really don't know why. Then my mother came up. She came upstairs, like she always did, she came in and she looked at me . . . and she knew. She knew. I have no doubt that she knew. And I looked at her and I said, "Mother, Henry came in here tonight and he . . ." And she cut me off right there, she just cut me off. She turned around and looked in the mirror and started fixing her hair and telling me what she'd had for dinner. She described the entire meal course by course. Rib roast and little potatoes and green beans and this marvelous dessert. And I was sitting there with the covers up around my neck, and I could hardly breathe. I wanted her to come over to me and to put her arms around me and to tell me that I wasn't a bad girl . . . that I wasn't a bad girl. And she tells me all about her meal!

STEPHANIE *wipes at her tears.* MAGGIE's *hand comes in from outside of frame and rests on* STEPHANIE's *shoulder.*

STEPHANIE: Well. And then she left my room. And she shut the door. And she'd never done that. She'd never shut the door before. It was as if somehow at that moment, the door was shut. It was extremely symbolic. And so I stayed there . . . here . . . that night. And I got up early the next morning, and I got on a bus and I went to Maggie's to the college. And I stayed in the dorm for three days. Just sitting there. And when I came home I put a lock on my door. She never asked me why.

MAGGIE *gathers* STEPHANIE *up in her arms, and holds her while she cries.*

FADE OUT

[handwritten margin note:] why can't the mother face this?

FADE IN:

15. Home Movie: Children's Parade   DAY/EXT.

Parade of children, each pushing a doll carriage or bicycle that has been decorated. The two Sisters have a doll carriage covered with handmade paper flowers. In the final image, they stand against a brick wall, holding giant lollipops—prize winners.

NARRATOR: (Over the home-movie images) Chatter. Long, long stories that are just a bunch of words strung together. Never the quick summation, never the one word that generalizes it all. Confusing stories that are really like the centers from five different stories. If there are associations they are so private that I can't possibly follow them. On the couch my mother sits and talks. I haven't seen her since she moved away. Two years, during which time I have been incredibly angry at her for so totally controlling me as a child, for not giving me the love in the way I wanted it, for not being the woman I wanted her to be, for teaching me to be weak. I expected my visit to be filled with anger; to my surprise it is not. It is sad. She is an angry, bitter woman whose life did not go at all the way she wanted it to. She sees her life as being over. She's just waiting to die, and all she wants is to have a little fun while she's waiting. It is this note of resignation about her which I find so difficult to face. It is Nancy who is angry, breaking everything in Mom's house. Platters disintegrate in her hands, glasses crack against the faucet as she washes them. I am not the angry one. I am filled with sadness and love for this woman who sits on the couch. And I want to be able to reach out and hand her the secret that will turn everything around, that will make her happy.

FADE OUT

FADE IN:

16. Bedroom. Mother's House   DAY/INT.

STEPHANIE *and* MAGGIE *sit at their mother's dressing table.* STEPHANIE *tries on lipstick.* MAGGIE, *bored, casually searches through the drawers.*

STEPHANIE: I can't imagine . . . she was that cheerleader, you remember her. I think she was in between us, you and me. Anyway, I saw her and I walked past and I said "Hello" and she didn't recognize me. And so she gave me one of those nice smiley faces that you give to people that you know you should know, but . . .

MAGGIE *pulls a bottle from the drawer and reads the label.*

MAGGIE: Three times a day as needed for depression.
STEPHANIE: What's that?
MAGGIE: Pills. Take one capsule at bedtime for sleep. Holy shit! It says "Refill as needed." She's been taking these since 1970. These are from '71. And they let her refill it . . . all this time, can you believe this?

Now STEPHANIE, *too, joins in on the search, rifling through the drug bottles in the drawer.*

STEPHANIE: Well, I knew that she had—had some stuff, but . . .
MAGGIE: Valium! Valium!
STEPHANIE: Maggie, everybody has Valium.
MAGGIE: I know, but it's so bad for you! Did you watch *60 Minutes?*

STEPHANIE *pulls out another bottle.*

STEPHANIE: Wow! Speed. I don't mean . . . they call it diet pills, but it's speed.
MAGGIE: Oh, that's great—Valium and speed! Sleeping pills and speed. Things for depression and speed.
STEPHANIE: Well I didn't know she was . . .

They pull open a second drawer and peek inside.

MAGGIE AND STEPHANIE: *Valley of the Dolls? Again Peyton Place!??*
STEPHANIE: She must have read the first *Peyton Place* then.

They start pulling paperback books from the drawer.

MAGGIE: This is the woman who reads *Reader's Digest?*
STEPHANIE: This is the woman who gets *Guiding Posts* from Covenant Homes? Oh my God. Have you read these? They're awful books.
MAGGIE: I saw this movie. It was an awful movie. Ohhhhh . . .

STEPHANIE *holds up a cassette tape she's just unearthed.*

STEPHANIE: I didn't realize she was into these things. What would she have a cassette for?
MAGGIE: Maybe that's a letter. People send letters that way. What's so funny? Is that so odd?

MAGGIE *moves over to search the desk. She pulls out a long white envelope.*

MAGGIE: Attorneys-at-Law? That's not her attorney. Look at that.

MAGGIE *holds the envelope up to the light.*

STEPHANIE: Is that Henry's attorney? I want to see what the settlement was.
MAGGIE: Yeah. It feels like money. It really feels like dollar bills.
STEPHANIE: Open it up.

MAGGIE *opens the envelope and peeks inside.*

MAGGIE: Money. Money in an envelope! I don't believe this. It's probably her Christmas money or something.
STEPHANIE: Money.
MAGGIE: Shhhhhh!
STEPHANIE: She's not going to hear me . . .

FADE OUT

FADE IN:

17. Home Movies: Montage   DAY/EXT.

Mother walking with her two Daughters: outside the house, on vacation, at the beach, at the school yard.

NARRATOR: (Over the home-movie images) We rented a car to drive around the is- land, passed a sign for a garage sale, stopped the car, and went in. Mom waited in the car. I came out with an old rayon Hawaiian shirt from the forties. What a find. It even fits me, which is a surprise since I'm so small. Mom took one look and went, "Oh, how can you stand the thought of wearing clothes someone else wore?" When we got back to her apartment, she took me into her bedroom and pulled out from her drawer a package all wrapped in tissue paper. "Maybe you'd like this. I've been saving it for thirty years. It was part of my trousseau. The only thing that is left." I gently unwrapped the package. It was a pair of pale pink silk pajamas. All trimmed in lace and satin. They were so beautiful it took my breath away. I tried them on. They fit perfectly. Snug, but not tight. Clinging to my body, hanging softly. I was shocked. I am so small, Mom so very large. She was once my size. I started to cry. For so many years she had kept this packed away in drawers and tissue paper, knowing she would never again fit into it. It was as if she was handing me, willing me, a little piece of her dreams. And I loved her very much for the gift.

FADE OUT

FADE IN:

18. Home Movies: Montage DAY/EXT.

Images of the Mother: with friends at the ocean, on vacation visiting historic sites, at home. In the final image, she puts her arm around her Daughter and walks with her across an empty field.

NARRATOR: (Over the home-movie images) Last night I dreamed. I am with Nancy. She is dying. She has cancer of the jaw. I go home to Mom. Nancy is there and asks to be killed. She says to set her on fire. I do, and she melts very slowly. It is terrifying to watch, especially her face melting. Mom is wonderful. She really helps, talking to Nancy as she burns, stoking the fire. All this goes on for a long time. Finally I cannot take it any longer. I tell her I have to go to class. I leave. Nancy is dead, but not totally burned up. I know I should stay 'til the very end, but I just can't. I leave and go walking along the lake through the marshes. I don't go to class. I need to be alone. I am scared and upset. I go home, hoping Nancy's body is gone. It is gone. Mom waited until it burned completely, then smashed it up and buried it in the marsh. She has done this terrible task so that I wouldn't have to do it. I am very grateful. I wander to her, she holds me in her arms, and I start to cry.

FADE OUT

19. Black Screen

NARRATOR: I imagine my mother seeing this, feeling the pain, eroding the pleasure. "Why do you have to say all this?" she asks. *quotation? →*

Credits

CHARACTER IMPROVISATIONS
Penelope Victor as MAGGIE
Anne Wilford as STEPHANIE
NARRATOR Jerri Hancock

SOUND AND CAMERA ASSISTANTS
Sharon Bement
Barbara Roos

GRAPHICS
Nancy Zucker

SPECIAL THANKS
Irene Wilford
Emily McKenty
Jerri Hancock

CLOSING QUOTATION FROM
Deena Metzger, "The Book of Hags," in *Sinister Wisdom* (fall 1976)

Written, directed, and edited by Michelle Citron. Copyright 1978 by
Michelle Citron.

What You Take For Granted . . .

A Film by Michelle Citron

NOTE: *This film uses three different visual styles: documentary montages of women on the job; talking-head interviews with women describing their work experiences; and a narrative of two of the interviewees—Anna, the truck driver, and Dianna, the doctor—developing a shaky friendship. Only the montages are authentic documentary. The six interviewees, including Anna and Dianna, are actors playing scripted roles. These six characters are a distillation of the thirty women interviewed for the film. These women are listed at the end of the screenplay. The question remains: Is there a difference between narrative fiction truth and documentary truth? And what are the differences between the private truths we tell ourselves and the public truths we tell others?*

FADE UP: **for Judy Hoffman and Sue Michmerhuizen**

OPENING TITLE: **What You Take For Granted . . .**

1. Montage
DAY/INT/EXT.

Chicago. Images of an industrial city. Workers make this city function: an engineer repairing an elevator; a printer; a house painter; a cable splicer, a worker repairing the utility lines; an airline pilot; a mail carrier; a firefighter; a laborer, digging holes; and a welder, high up on an iron girder. All women.

2. The Doctor   DAY/INT.

DIANNA, *a poised woman in her late thirties, sits on a couch in a middle-class living room and tells her story directly into the lens of the camera.*

DIANNA: I had always had this fantasy of what it meant to be a doctor, which I guess was derived in part from my father and in part from all those TV series I watched when I was growing up. The thing about medicine is that it's useful. You can't really argue with whether it's socially valid or not. And this fantasy, this fantasy included being listened to and intervening in people's lives . . . all for the good. And that's a very potent fantasy for a woman.

3. The Artist   DAY/INT.

The ARTIST *is gray haired, in her midsixties. She talks standing in her kitchen, animated and intense. Plants, sculptures, knickknacks are everywhere.*

ARTIST: All my life I'd been interested in art so I decided I was going to enroll at the university near the small farming community where I lived. And I did that and I became interested in sculpture. Welding. And that's what I do. Almost everything I do is welded. And it looks easy, you know, and it isn't. It's hard and it takes hours and hours because you're dealing with materials that are obstinate and obdurate and unyielding and hard. And you have to be real careful not to blow yourself up, too.

4. The Carpenter   DAY/INT.

The CARPENTER *sits in her living room, a picture of her young daughter framed behind her. She's direct and charming, in her late twenties.*

CARPENTER: There are about twenty-five women out of twenty-five thousand carpenters in Chicago. It's something we chose, but it's not ideal.

5. The Professor

The PROFESSOR teaches philosophy at the university. She's in her mid-forties, regal and proud. She sits in her study, surrounded by books.

PROFESSOR: One of the things I find interesting about being an intellectual is that I spent all those years, reading all those books about white men and the journeys of white men. Knowing that I needed to speak that language, yet also knowing that world was not about me.

6. The Cable Splicer

The CABLE SPLICER talks to us from her living-room couch. Mid-twenties, blond and perky, she looks like a sorority girl.

CABLE SPLICER: There are about seven women cable splicers in my garage and we're the ones that go into the manholes and up on the poles laying cable for the public utilities. And we thought as more and more women got to be hired that they would continue all the way, and maybe even get to be a fifty-fifty ratio. Men and women. But they hired seven women, that was the magic number. That was the quota for the government. When they hit that number they stopped.

7. The Truck Driver

ANNA sits at the table in her bright yellow kitchen. In her mid-thirties, her hands move as much as her mouth.

ANNA: None of my friends went to college when I was in high school. But I got this scholarship, I guess I got good grades for some reason. I got this scholarship to this school, Schimer College. I went there for about a semester and I found it totally boring. So, I came back to Chicago and got a job in this big national insurance company. As a secretary. It wasn't really a secretary, it was more like a file clerk, transferring numbers from one page to another. It was more boring than you can possibly imagine. One day I'm looking through this company newsletter and I see this full-page ad of a woman hanging off a truck with the company logo on it . . . saying there's new opportunities for women truckers. So I thought, shit, this could be a piece of cake.

8. The Doctor   DAY/INT.

The interview continues.

DIANNA: I started medical school in 1966. And at that time there were five of us in the class. After the first year, two women were asked to stay back and one was asked to leave. Percentagewise, that was just incredibly high. And it happened in every class. You couldn't quite figure out how they got you. But one thing was that you always stood out. In a lecture, if one of the men wasn't there it was never noticed. But if one of us wasn't there it was like a neon sign flashing "Absent." I had this best friend in college who had better grades than I did and scored higher on her medical boards. And she was denied admission to any medical school. I went through a lot of searching about why was I the one who was let in? What did it mean that I fit some male admissions officer's image of what a woman doctor ought to be like? Why was I the one that was okay?

9. The Artist   DAY/INT.

The interview continues.

ARTIST: For years and years I waitressed . . . just trying to get along . . . trying to survive and trying to figure out what to do with my life and raise my children.

10. The Carpenter   DAY/INT.

The interview continues.

CARPENTER: People have this glorified idea about carpentry, construction work, whatever, this fantasy for a woman. But it's really hard work. And we got into it because we had no choice. It was either shit

---

women's work for shit pay or shit men's work for more pay. And I'm a single parent, so money's important to me.

11. The Doctor DAY/INT.

The interview continues.

DIANNA: There's a real male camaraderie that exists in medical school, and it has to exist if you're going to survive. There was this guy in my class when I was in my first year who was heartsick over this woman in Minneapolis. He was practically flunking out and the woman's mother didn't want her to get married, which was what he wanted. I'd say 90 percent of the freshman class marched practically en masse to Minneapolis to plead with this girl's mother to let her be married. Let her sacrifice her daughter so this guy could pull himself out of his slump. And it worked. You know, they were married, she moved back to Chicago, he began to get straight As. It was this real success story.

12. The Truck Driver DAY/INT.

The interview continues.

ANNA: They would lift these huge loaded mailbags . . . and try and swing them around and hit me. I mean, shit like this was going on. They'd say things like, "My wife is in the hospital having our third baby and I'm letting the dishes pile up because that's woman's work." Or they'd draw cocks and balls in the grime on my truck window. I mean, stuff like this was happening all the time . . . I got this attitude that I could stand in shit up to my eyeballs and not let anything affect me. You know, I was in my lock device. 'Cause I wasn't gonna let them scare me off. And that was good for me. I needed to do that.

FADE OUT

FADE UP:

13. Montage DAY/INT.

Hands at work: inking the printing rollers; scraping old paint; tightening gears with a wrench; making chain link on the line.

14. Anna's House. Kitchen. DAY/INT.

The narrative begins . . . DIANNA *follows* ANNA *into her kitchen.*

ANNA: Thank you for coming.
DIANNA: You're welcome.
ANNA: I ripped open my hand a little bit.
DIANNA: Did you wash it off?

DIANNA *takes off her jacket and pulls some first-aid supplies from her bag.* ANNA *hangs over the sink.*

ANNA: Like you told me. I hate hospitals. I really appreciate this.

DIANNA *joins her at the sink.*

DIANNA: Let's see.
ANNA: Not too bad, huh?
DIANNA: No. Let's wash it off a little.

DIANNA *cleans the wound as they get to know each other.*

ANNA: I don't usually cut myself this way.
DIANNA: How'd you get my number?
ANNA: It's in the book. So's your name.

DIANNA *seems dumbfounded by the simplicity of it all.*

DIANNA: It's deep. And it's in an awkward place. I think I'm going to put a couple of stitches in, okay? I think it would be best.
ANNA: I have stitchaphobia. I mean, can't you do like one of those butterflies? You know, I can't stand with the stitches.

DIANNA: Okay. Let me try. If it works, fine. If not, then we'll go to stitches. Come on and sit down . . . will you hold that a second? You've got to keep this clean, okay?

DIANNA *dresses the wound.*

ANNA: It's beautiful. You're a real doctor.

DIANNA *works efficiently as she makes small talk.*

DIANNA: That's what they tell me. Okay. Now . . . did you have dinner yet?
ANNA: I was making it when I cut myself. I'm pretty nauseous. For me to lose my appetite is something.

ANNA *is a bit agitated and distracted.* DIANNA *looks around. Dirty dishes, dinner half-made on the stove.*

DIANNA: Looks pretty good over there. You know what? I think I'm going to go on and make you some dinner.
ANNA: Forget it.
DIANNA: No. It's okay. Eggs, and . . .
ANNA: No. Really, listen . . . I have a refrigerator full of beer. I'll order in pizza.
DIANNA: I want to. I want to eat it with you. Okay? I'll stay for dinner. I'm really happy to.

DIANNA *picks up an onion and starts to peel it.*

ANNA: This is nuts. You don't have to fix my hand and make me dinner.
DIANNA: That's all right. So what's it like to drive a truck?

15. The Truck Driver   DAY/INT.

The interview resumes.

ANNA: Actually, once I started getting used to the job I was just this eager beaver around town. You know, I was just making points for myself everywhere . . . see because the people that I delivered to were not directly threatened by a female's presence being a truck driver. So, my boss would get phone calls all the time saying how I was cheery and lifting my load . . . I was so thrilled just to get some good feelings from people on my route after what would occur every morning that I was in seventh heaven.

16. The Artist   DAY/INT.

The interview continues.

ARTIST: Nineteen sixty-seven I think it was, '67, '68. Another woman and I entered a competition at the school and there were about fifty-three people who entered the competition and we were the only women and we won first and second place. But they wouldn't let us have all the money. This is an honest-to-God story. They kept most of the money. They let us have the money for materials, but they wouldn't give us the prize money. I'll never forget it. I went up there. I was all dressed up. And they said, "Is this for your husband?" And I said, "No. I don't have a husband. *My* name is Chris Reilly." And the guy went "Oh." It was funny. Even then I knew that.

17. The Professor   DAY/INT.

The interview continues.

PROFESSOR: You have to be twice as good to get any place, but if you're very good the men you work with might become threatened. You walk a very fine line, and your success depends on someone else's assessment of your work. Now this is true of men, too, but they're judged truly by their peers in a way that women and blacks, at least at this point in history, are not.

18. Chicago Alley   DAY/EXT.

A sunny, warm fall day—perfect for winterizing the car. The hood is up and ANNA *leans into the motor. She picks up a socket wrench and pulls a spark plug.*

DIANNA *comes jogging down the alley.*

DIANNA: Anna. Hi.

ANNA *looks up, surprised.*

ANNA: Hey. Hi.
DIANNA: How are you?

ANNA: Fine.

DIANNA: How's your hand?

ANNA *wipes it on a rag and inspects it. The bandage is black with grease and dirt.*

DIANNA: Oh God.

ANNA: This grease is good for it.

DIANNA: Oh yeah? I won't look. What are you doing?

ANNA: Just changing the plugs, greasing up the parts, changing the oil, you know . . .

ANNA *continues to work as she talks.*

DIANNA: I don't know really.

ANNA: So what are you doing?

DIANNA: I'm out running.

ANNA: How far do you run a day?

DIANNA: I do about four miles every three days.

ANNA: That's great. I do five. But slow. I need to run. But I haven't run in a long time.

DIANNA: Do you want to run next Wednesday? Do you have off?

ANNA: Yeah, I don't work till three.

DIANNA: Great. We could run in the morning.

ANNA: Okay. Great.

DIANNA: Listen, I've got to keep moving. Will you give me a call? Wednesday morning?

ANNA: Yeah.

DIANNA'S *off and running.*

DIANNA: Terrific.

19. The Truck Driver   DAY/INT.

The interview resumes.

ANNA: One day last year a woman came up to me and said, "Anna, I've gotta thank you because I realize that you opened this whole thing up. Because of you, things are real easy around here. And I was really blown away. For having a little bit of appreciation happen. Not that I think I'm a saint or anything, but I'll tell you, for five years, even now . . . there was no glory in it. It was really lonely.

20. The Carpenter   DAY/INT.

The interview continues.

CARPENTER: My best friend on the job is this older black man. He's the only black man on the site because until recently the trades have been very closed to black people. I mean, other than myself, he's the only other black carpenter that I know. The first day on the site he whispered to me, "I know you can do this job. My mother worked in the cotton fields for fifty years. I know women can work hard." He's the best carpenter on the job. And I could learn a lot from him. That is, when I get a chance to work with him.

21. The Cable Splicer   DAY/INT.

The interview continues.

CABLE SPLICER: I was the second woman hired in my garage. Karen was the first. And naturally we wanted to work together. There was sort of a camaraderie just because we were the only two women in the garage. And they wouldn't let us at first. When we finally got to work together they pitted us up against each other. They would give us both difficult jobs to do and it was a real competitive thing about who could do a better job. You know, one was expected to do one better than the other. But what we would do is both of us would go do her job and then both of us would go do my job.

22. The Artist   DAY/INT.

The interview continues.

ARTIST: So when I moved to the city I thought, "Oh, this is going to be better. Bigger shop, better school, better shop." No way. Because the guys wouldn't talk to me. None of them would talk to me. Like for months. I went around and was lonely.

And then one day this guy, a graduate student, started to talk to me. And we're friends to this day and I swear it's because he started to communicate. And he wasn't like the other guys. He wasn't macho. He was considerate, and he was kind. And he couldn't understand what these other guys were doing. And the other men thought he was effeminate, and they thought he was queer. And he got to play the outcast of the group. That is until I came along. Then I got to play that role. And then there was the bully. There is always a bully, right? And his name was David. And he was a real pain in the ass, let me tell you. One day I was in there welding and he came in and he had this way of laying his stuff out. Laying it out all over everything. Taking up my space. I backed up into some of his material and I cut my arm rather badly. I was just bleeding all over the place. And I had to go and take stitches. And I was getting very, very angry at him. And I was angry at myself for letting him do that to me. So, I came back to the shop, I remember, and he was talking with one of his friends, and he looked up at me and he said, rather contemptuously, "What's the matter with you?" And I said to myself, "Chris, you've raised your kids all by yourself. You've put yourself through art school alone. You've served thousands of people and waitressed hundreds and hundreds of dinners. And you're gonna let this little worm make you miserable?" And that really did it. That's what did it. And I said to him, "You motherfucking son-of-a-bitch, you come over here and I'll kill you." And he said, "Calm down, Chris." I was really angry. He knew it. And I said, "You son-of-a-bitch, you come over here and I'll kill you." You know he got really scared. He got really frightened. And I remember I said it three times. I said, "You know, you're the most inconsiderate son-of-a-bitch I've ever known. You don't deserve to live on this earth. Come over here and I'll kill you." And I didn't care anymore. I would have done it. And you know what? He changed. In an instant, he changed.

23. City Park

DAY/EXT.

The sun glistens off the water. DIANNA *and* ANNA *stretch, prior to running.*

ANNA: What are you doing, Dianna?
DIANNA: I'm stretching the backs of my legs.
ANNA: But don't bounce. You really shouldn't be bouncing.

DIANNA: Why not?
ANNA: You're gonna screw up all your lumbars back there.

DIANNA: Really?

ANNA: You never bounce a muscle. You just hold tight with it. Breathe in through the nose, out through the mouth. Don't they teach you that in doctor school?

DIANNA: No. There's no courses in running. Or stretching. I always do that.

ANNA: You're gonna really screw up your back.

DIANNA: How do you know about backs?

ANNA: I'm a truck driver. That's the first thing that screws you up. Your back . . . You want to do it?

DIANNA: Yeah.

ANNA: Let's go. Five? Slow.

DIANNA: All right.

And with that, they're off.

24. Park. Later.   DAY/EXT.

ANNA *and* DIANNA *sit by the water's edge.* DIANNA *munches on a pear as they talk.*

ANNA: God. I'm so stiff. I haven't run in like five days. I was running like five miles every day with my friend Czar. And he sprained his leg.

DIANNA: With who?

ANNA: Czar. The Czar of Chicago. That's what I call him. His name is Caesar.

DIANNA: Who is he?

ANNA: He's a cook in this greasy spoon that I frequent. And he makes a real mean scrambled egg. And we fuck around, you know.

DIANNA: You don't live with him, do you?

ANNA: Oh, God, not Czar. What about you? Are you living with someone?

DIANNA *stops eating; she's obviously uncomfortable with the question.*

DIANNA: No. Not anymore.

ANNA: So you were?

ANNA *takes the pear from* DIANNA'S *hand and bites.*

DIANNA: Yeah, I was.

In an effort of conciliation, ANNA *offers the pear back to* DIANNA.

ANNA: Want some?

DIANNA *takes it.*

ANNA: Okay. So tell Anna the story. Who was he? Sounds like heartbreak hotel or something.

DIANNA *thinks a moment before answering. When she does, she looks* ANNA *directly in the eye . . . a challenge.*

DIANNA: He was a she.
ANNA: Hm.

For a moment ANNA *is at a loss for words. But only for a moment.*

ANNA: Are you gay or something?
DIANNA: Yeah.
ANNA: (*She thinks about it for a moment.*) Far fuckin' out . . . so who was she?
DIANNA: She's another doctor where I work.
ANNA: How long did you live together?
DIANNA: Fifteen months. Exactly.
ANNA: Doctors count in months. The baby's not a year and a half, the baby's fifteen months. So um, what happened?
DIANNA: It just didn't work out.
ANNA: Did she leave you, or did you leave her?

ANNA *just won't let up.* DIANNA *gets more and more uncomfortable by the second.*

DIANNA: It just didn't work out.
ANNA: One of you fell out of love? That what happen? Or was there another person involved?
DIANNA: You know, I'm starting to feel like I'm being interviewed.
ANNA: I'm sorry.
DIANNA: It's okay.
ANNA: I've got such a mouth. I'm just open, just curious, you know. I'm sorry.
DIANNA: It's okay.

But it's not really. > how is this shown?

25. The Cable Splicer   DAY/INT.

The interview continues.

CABLE SPLICER: I didn't really understand that when you start a job, any job, you go through a period of initiation. Kind of paying your dues. And really proving yourself in the job. I assumed I was being treated in a certain way because I was a woman. You might be asked to stay late one day, or when the guys go out to lunch I had to stay and clean out the truck. Just little things. You know you do that extra stuff and <u>you earn your position. You earn their respect,</u> basically. And when I started to apprentice people, I thought "I'll do it differently." I thought I would give them all kinds of good feedback and be a little bit more open and understanding about them starting in a position. And I basically got walked over. You really can't do it that way. I find now when I apprentice people I put them pretty much through the same stuff that I went through.

26. The Professor   DAY/INT.

The interview continues.

PROFESSOR: I think it would be helpful if there were women who told you how to survive. Who said, "They're going to do this and they'll try to do that. You have to move this way, this way, and this way." Some of us are in that position now. But I think it's an erroneous assumption we're making if we think that these women are going to readily accept our help and regard us with the same kind of respect that they have for men.

27. The Carpenter   DAY/INT.

The interview continues.

CARPENTER: Sometimes you can find different ways of doing things. Like carrying heavy pieces of lumber, for instance, they're four-by-six-by-sixteen. And they're heavy and they're unwieldy. And the men carry them on their shoulders. Well, I have a small upper body so I carry them on my hips. Now the men can't teach me that. It's something that I just had to find out for myself. Now, as women carpenters we have to find our own advantages.

28. Dianna's House. Study.

DIANNA *talks on the phone, an ironing board set up in front of her.* ANNA *sits at the desk doodling. She occasionally glances up at* DIANNA.

DIANNA: What medication is he on? . . . Uh, uh. No, just restart the IV until the morning when the service comes on. Ah, uh . . . Sure . . . bye . . .

She hangs up the phone and goes back to ironing her shirt.

DIANNA: I'm sorry, that's going to happen all night because I'm on call . . . So, she wants to be a carpenter? That sounds great.
ANNA: I don't think it sounds great at all. I spent the whole conversation trying to talk her out of it.
DIANNA: Why not? You do it, Anna.
ANNA: I know I do it, but it doesn't mean I want her to do it. I mean, she's young enough. I want her to make something of herself.
DIANNA: Yeah, but I think she really sees all the stuff that you've gotten from your job and she wants some of that.
ANNA: She doesn't see what I have from my job at all.
DIANNA: Look, I know it's hard, but look at all the stuff that you've demystified, all the stuff you know how to do. She understands that, she wants a piece of that.
ANNA: Listen, toots, driving a truck is about as mystifying as ironing or something. I mean, she sees it as a fantasy, this whole thing. She doesn't understand. I want her to go to school (*phone RINGS*) . . . I want her to . . .

The phone RINGS persistently, interrupting ANNA *in midsentence. The intrusion annoys her.*

DIANNA: Hello . . . Yeah. Well who wrote that script? . . . That combination isn't as bad as some others, but somebody is going to be in a lot of trouble tomorrow . . . no, I want you to watch her tonight . . . If you see Mac I want you to tell him to call me right away . . . uh, uh, okay . . . bye.

DIANNA *hangs up the phone and goes back to her ironing.*

ANNA: I don't know, I want her to go back to school because I want her to feel—

DIANNA: —I think it's crazy for her to go back to school. She should just be out there in the world and doing a job.

Now ANNA'S *getting really annoyed.*

ANNA: There's no power out there in the world doing a job. I hear you on the phone, "Tell Mac to call me back." You know, there's no Mac that calls me back.

DIANNA: I know that I have something of a privileged life, but I also know that I don't have the kind of power that you think I have. You really think that I have it very easy and I have all this power on my job. I don't. I have lots of problems where I work. I take a lot of shit. And it's not easy.

ANNA: Not too many problems that $60,000 a year couldn't fix.

RING! RING! The shrill RING of the phone interrupts her yet again . . .

DIANNA: Hello . . . Yeah . . . What's the peak flow? . . . Yeah . . . Is he on steroids? . . . When was the last dose of aminophylline? . . . Umm . . . How much does he weigh? . . . Okay, what I want you to do is . . . Yeah, just two hundred milliliters of aminophylline . . .

In a huff, ANNA *gets up and leaves.* DIANNA, *caught on the phone, can only wave a feeble good-bye.*

29. The Carpenter   DAY/INT.

The interview continues.

CARPENTER: If you work five years you make union scale. If you work twenty years you make union scale. Our pay never increases. The only increase we do get is once a year at contract negotiation. This year we got 10 percent. Now that doesn't keep up with inflation. And $15.40 is all we ever make. We don't get paid vacations. We don't get time off. If I'm sent home in the middle of the day, I don't get paid. If it rains and I have to go home, I don't get paid. If I drive an hour to work and an hour home, at that point sometimes I've lost money.

30. The Cable Splicer

DAY/INT.

The interview continues.

CABLE SPLICER: There was pretty much a buddy system in the place when we started there, and we just didn't understand it at all. You might be on the job and ask the foreman if you can go to the farmers' market or go to the cleaners or do something for your own personal benefit, and he would let you do it. In return you might have to work overtime. Or you would do him a favor. And the first time I was asked to work overtime I went in waving the rule book, all pissed off, saying I don't have to do this. I got all bent out of shape. It wasn't that I didn't want to do it. I didn't understand. I didn't know that if I did him a favor he'd do me a favor later on.

31. The Carpenter

DAY/INT.

The interview continues.

CARPENTER: I have noticed that the men asked for help more and more. Like carrying a piece of plywood. And I think that's good. And I think the women have done that.

32. The Truck Driver

DAY/INT.

ANNA'S *interview resumes.*

ANNA: I think the most stressful part of the job is the fact that we're always on call. They call me up at eleven or twelve at night and tell me to come in to do another shift when I've already been in there doing a shift that day. The hours are so irregular I have insomnia now. I've learned the value of these modular phones, you know, that you can unplug.

33. Anna's House. Living Room.   NIGHT/INT.

The living room is dark. The key turns in the door and ANNA *walks in, sorting through her mail. She hangs her jacket on the doorknob. She disappears into the kitchen and returns chugging a beer.*

She goes over to the couch and lights a cigarette. She takes a puff, then picks up her clarinet and wets the reed. She puts the clarinet to her lips and plays a soulful, lonely tune.

34. The Truck Driver   DAY/INT.

ANNA'S *interview resumes.*

ANNA: People say that if you work four years outside, you can never go back inside. And I really think that there's truth to that. Because, like out on the road, it's so intoxicating just covering all that space. A hundred twenty-five miles all around the state. I roll down the window. I put on a jazz station or a blues station or classical, whatever . . . You know, bopping around. I go home and drop off my laundry, I do shopping. There's a sense of outwitting the company. And I was making good money. You know, there were really good parts to it.

35. The Cable Splicer   DAY/INT.

The interview continues. The CABLE SPLICER *is seen in long shot and we finally see that she's very pregnant—eight months.*

CABLE SPLICER: We had to go into a certain alley on a Saturday morning. And everybody was out in the alley. The guys are all out there working on their cars. You know, the place was just packed. So we pull up in the truck—I'm with this other guy who's not my regular partner. And I go up in the bucket. And he's down in the truck feeding me cable. And all of a sudden I hear a lot of noise down beneath me. Right underneath me, there's a fight breaking out. And I know this guy

I'm working with is starting to panic. And so, I look down and he splits. So I grab one of the manhole hooks and I get myself down and I get out of the bucket. And I basically have to break it up. There's a couple of Latino guys, I speak some Spanish so I'm yelling at them in Spanish. And getting them to cool out. That's the best thing to do. You don't want to call the cops in a situation like that. I don't want to be known as the one who calls the cops.

36. The Truck Driver   DAY/INT.

The interview continues.

ANNA: Safety in our company is a joke. I mean, when I first got trained they showed us films and slides and we had lectures about what it is to be safe and all these things like . . . I couldn't wear sneakers, I couldn't wear a certain jacket I wanted to, I had to learn how to do the windows. Everything was for utmost safety. But when it came to some conditions, they didn't care at all about safety. They would have us driving through the thickest fog. Sleet, hail, rain, you know. They had us go through the blizzard of '78. On glare ice. Even when the roads were closed by the state police, we were limping around. I remember working that night and it took me four hours to do a forty-five-minute job. And then they'd send the next shift out after us. They don't care. They say they care about safety, but they don't care about safety. They care about money.

37. The Doctor   DAY/INT.

DIANNA'S *interview continues.*

DIANNA: In medical school, on rotation, I would also be the only woman with eight men. And it was really hard for me because I didn't know how I was supposed to act. You know, I didn't get it. And the men would be standing around and discussing the patient as if they were invisible, and I'd be putting up the bed rail or explaining a procedure or asking them if they were comfortable or not. And I realized that I was approaching the whole thing like I was a nurse, like my mother, except that I was a doctor.

38. Dianna's Kitchen

In the late hours of the night, DIANNA *mops her kitchen floor. She leans over the bucket and squeezes out the mop. The phone RINGS and she picks up.*

DIANNA: Hello . . . Hi, Daddy . . . No, I'm still up. I'm mopping my floor . . . Oh, you got my letter . . . What do you think? . . . Why? . . . I don't think you need to be concerned, it's a very good place to work . . . No, it's really a good job . . . I've given it a lot of thought . . . I haven't said yes yet, but I'm going to . . . I don't want to go into private practice . . . I know. I'm sure he's a great doctor, but I couldn't, I don't even like him . . . I could never work for him . . . No, it's really what I want to do . . . County is a very respectable place to work, a lot of my peers work there . . . I don't think it's the same thing . . . No, it's not like when I left medical school . . . I don't feel like I'm blowing it, I feel like I'm doing something that I really believe in, I have this—I have this opportunity to work . . . Why? . . . No, Daddy . . . Uh-huh . . . I'm never gonna get married . . . Uh-huh . . . Listen I've got to go now . . . Please tell Mom that I send my love, okay? . . . Next week I will . . . Okay . . . Bye.

She hangs up the phone and just stands there, too upset to move.

39. The Doctor

DIANNA'S *interview resumes.*

DIANNA: I realized that if I could just force myself not to smile when I talked, it set off this chain reaction of a different body language. My expression changed, my voice lowered, and my stance was different. I was amazed that it worked. Something as simple as not smiling. But you know, you don't want to have to do it that way. I just want to say, "Look, you know, we're in this together, I want this and you want that, and let's just figure out how to do it." But you can't do that by yourself.

40. The Professor   DAY/INT.

The interview continues.

PROFESSOR: I sometimes see women being the victim with men. You'll never get what you want that way. They do what I call fogging. And I think that women do this because they don't know how to deal with the structures that exist. Instead of challenging them they just go away. It used to happen to me. Suddenly I just wouldn't be there anymore. I think, in part, it's not wanting to deal with your anger. It's much easier to fog than to be angry. Or to take responsibility for what your perceptions are. Or to take risks.

41. The Artist   DAY/INT.

The interview continues.

ARTIST: Our society is so fragmented, it expects passive women and killer men. You know, I think sometimes that women can get by much more easily than men in being whole. Simply because we are not taken so seriously. I believe in that area, men have it much more difficult. You know, the gentle men I know have been far more destroyed than the tough women.

42. The Carpenter   DAY/INT.

The interview continues.

CARPENTER: This job is very difficult if you're a single parent. I remember when I worked in an office, one day they were going to take out the phones. And the women just stormed into the manager's office and said, "What do you mean no phones? We have kids at home and they have to call us." Now that's one of the fringe benefits of that type of job.

43. The Cable Splicer

DAY/INT.

The interview continues.

CABLE SPLICER: I worked outside on the poles up until my fifth month. The only reason I really came in was just 'cause the weather got really bad. And then I went inside to a clerical job. They can't make you stop working because pregnancy is covered in our contract, and the clericals have the same contract as the craftspeople. So I could go inside at the same rate of pay. And I'll probably work right up until I deliver. And then afterwards I'll take a six-weeks paid leave of absence. You have the option of taking a six-months leave of absence, which I won't take advantage of because right now my husband's not employed and we really need the money. Actually, the hardest part's not been the pregnancy. I think it will be afterwards, because there is no provision in the company for day care.

44. The Carpenter

DAY/INT.

The interview continues.

CARPENTER: The morning times are really hard if you're a single parent. Let's face it. It's a lot easier if you have someone to get up to fix your breakfast and make you lunch. Like, this guy I work with told me, "I told my wife she has to get up and make my breakfast and make my lunch or I'm not bringing home the check. I'm not going to work. So, we need the money, so I work." So I said, "Does your wife work?" He said, "Yeah, she works part time." Now she only works six hours a day, plus taking care of the kids, plus fixing his breakfast and lunch. But she doesn't work as hard as we do. Ha!

45. The Truck Driver

DAY/INT.

The interview continues.

ANNA: The company thinks that because you get a living wage and good benefits that you owe your life to them. It's not a nine-to-five job. Talking about it now I realize why there's so much stress and tension between all the drivers working there because we're all hooked into everyone's pattern. Because if someone doesn't come in, you've got to work their shift. So there's this tension of dependency. And the whole thing is, if you're feeling sick, you're out on the road and you're feeling sick, you can't come back in. You can't say, "I'm sick, I want to go home." You're two-hundred miles from home and you just gotta keep going.

46. Dianna's Backyard   DAY/EXT.

DIANNA *pots plants while* ANNA *drinks a beer and keeps her company.* ANNA'S *very hyped up . . . and a bit drunk.*

ANNA: They usually just promote. And they have to hire a woman. Why? Why do they?

DIANNA: Why do they have to hire a woman?

ANNA: I'm glad you asked that. My friend in personnel says that the EEOC is wondering why all these women in these nontraditional jobs are cool enough to get in, but not to get out of the basement. You know that we're all skilled. Anyway, they have burned us, this company has burned us for so long even the EEOC can't ignore the smell. And I'm telling you that I have the most seniority. I know the job. And they have to hire a woman because they will be in big trouble if they don't, believe me.

DIANNA: And you're the best woman they could ever hire.

ANNA: Dig, dig, dig . . .

She takes another gulp of beer.

DIANNA: This is great.

ANNA: I know. I had this fight with Czar. I told him this last night. And he says that he can't stand anything that smacks of bosses. And I said, "Listen, it's not a question of boss here, it's a question of competency."

DIANNA: And you being recognized.

ANNA: Do you know what this means? I feel that if it happens, no more third shift. No more pulling doubles. No more boredom. No more insomnia, for heaven's sake. No more drugs, maybe, but you never know . . .

DIANNA: What?

ANNA: No, I don't know.

DIANNA: It's great.

ANNA: I know. I know.

DIANNA: I'm real excited for you.

ANNA: Will you drink for me?

DIANNA: Drink for you? I'll drink to you.

She clinks her Coke can against ANNA'S *beer can.*

ANNA: To Miss Boss.

47. The Carpenter   DAY/INT.

The interview continues.

CARPENTER: I always thought, "I'm gonna make a good carpenter." I'm pretty smart. I can figure things out. Mentally deal with problems. I'm very good at math. But the work is becoming more routinized, less skilled. The thinking part is being separated out more and more from the physical part. And we're at a disadvantage not being as strong. But on the other hand, the women are more together. We're very serious about becoming good carpenters.

48. The Doctor   DAY/INT.

DIANNA'S *interview resumes.*

DIANNA: I really wanted to work much more in concert with other people. Making decisions collectively and sharing the responsibility. And that just doesn't work in a hierarchy. And the other thing was that I wasn't meeting the traditional expectations of decisive behavior from a doctor. I felt like I was breaking new ground. But what it was seen as being was wishy-washy and weak. And indecisive.

49. The Artist   DAY/INT.

The interview continues.

ARTIST: I've seen too many women lose the soft, gentle parts of themselves and become just as gnarled up emotionally and tormented as men. It's much easier just to cut yourself off. And imitate. Imitate the aggressor. Imitate the men. Then you'll get the power. Then you'll get the raises and the promotions.

50. The Professor

The interview continues.

PROFESSOR: And I will always be different from my colleagues because I've had different reactions to the same experiences because I view them from a different perspective. And I will always be different from women who work in traditionally female roles. It has something to do with being in three worlds. Being a woman. Being a black woman. And working in a white male world. You see how it moves. You're not stuck in one place or another. There is this fantasy of an integrated life. And we think that we're split and white men have this wholeness. But that's a myth, too. Where are they whole? They are never forced to see the world other than from their own perspective. And if we're not careful we spend our whole lives thinking something's wrong with us.

51. Dianna's Study

NIGHT/INT.

DIANNA *is deep at work at her desk. She's interrupted by a persistent KNOCK, KNOCK, KNOCKING at her door.*

DIANNA: Okay. Okay.

She pushes up from her desk and goes to see who it is. When she opens the door, there stands ANNA.

ANNA: Dianna.
DIANNA: Anna.

ANNA *is quite drunk. She pushes her way in.*

ANNA: Hi. How are you? Oh, you're not sleeping.

DIANNA *leads the way back to her study, and plops down at her desk.*

DIANNA: No, I'm not. I'm in the middle of working, and I'm real hassled. You can only stay for a couple of minutes.

ANNA: Great. Great. Wow, you're all up here. I expected you . . . Well, I expected you . . . I didn't really expect you to be asleep but . . .
DIANNA: I'm working. I'm in the middle . . .

ANNA *picks up some papers from the desk and scans them.*

ANNA: What are you doing? God, your desk is such a mess.
DIANNA: I'm doing a lecture series on social medicine.
ANNA: Now that sounds intense.
DIANNA: (*Taking the papers from* ANNA'S *hands*) I really need this stuff to be here now.

ANNA *just picks up something else off the desk.*

ANNA: God, you know there's something about these medical journals. I was thinking about them the last time I was here . . .

She flips through a journal and stops.

ANNA: Oh my God, a large, lobated, pale, rectoral . . .

DIANNA *pulls the journal from her friend's hands.*

DIANNA: Anna, what's up?

The question is just the opening she needs.

ANNA: Oh God. It has been so rough. I can't tell you. Listen to this. You know, Monday they had me working on first shift. You know, they said, "Okay, first shift on all week." Then Tuesday I come in and they go, "No, we don't need you until second." And then what happens? Okay, I do second, big deal, it's still in the day, right? Then this guy gets sick and doesn't show up for third. I've got to work fucking second and third. And then first again Wednesday. And like I'm a maniac. I'm like a wild zombie. I really can't believe it . . . You know, so I've been trying to get to sleep, and my mind is like wandering . . .

ANNA *pulls a pack of cigarettes from her pocket.*

DIANNA: You can't smoke here now. I've got a real headache.
ANNA: Oh, sure.

She pockets the cigarettes.

DIANNA: I've got too much to do, you know?
ANNA: Really. It's hard all over. This is how it is. Oh God, so anyway. I told my boss. Fuck. I'm not going to work these fucking third shifts anymore

because I can't get to sleep. So, what I came here to ask is . . . if you know of something that could help me to sleep.

ANNA *plops down right on the desktop.*

DIANNA: Yeah, I do.

ANNA: You do? Great.

DIANNA: Yeah, I always do chamomile tea. And you can do calcium, too, if you're having a hard time.

ANNA: Are you kidding?

DIANNA: No. Honest.

ANNA: You mean inject calcium right into the cortex? That's what I'd have to do. I can't take no herbs and shit.

DIANNA: Look. Lie down in your bed. Drink some tea, breathe in and out.

ANNA: I don't believe in herbs.

DIANNA: Believe. It will work.

She goes back to her work, only half-listening to ANNA.

ANNA: What I'm asking . . . Listen. I've got an iron tank for a system here. You know what I'm saying? That stuff just doesn't cut it for me. I've been drinking tequila and reciting Cervantes all evening in the bar. They practically threw me out. I'm too exhausted to even play my clarinet. Listen. What I really need is a script for, you know, a Valium or some barbiturate.

This gets DIANNA's *attention.*

DIANNA: A Valium? Come on Anna. I'm not going to give you that crap.

ANNA: What do you mean? Everyone's on Valium. It's even on TV.

DIANNA: Well, not in my circles.

ANNA: Valium. Valium.

DIANNA: It's rotten for you.

ANNA: Don't you give it to patients?

DIANNA: You're not my patient.

ANNA: But I'd like to be.

DIANNA: Well, the doctor's not on call right now.

ANNA: (*with sarcasm*) Well, the doctor's not on call right now. Look at that. I mean, I don't see why you think it's so bad for me. Valium's just a fucking muscle relaxer.

DIANNA: I know what it is, Anna.

ANNA: Why are you playing God? Does it seem like I'm taking advantage of you here? Coming here and saying, "Doctor, give it to me." And if you don't do it I won't be your friend? I'm sorry. I'm really sorry. I asked you for something to break this fucking cycle. 'Cause if I fall asleep on the road, if they ask me to do third again . . . If they ask me to do third again. What am I going to do? Look at these bags. Doc. Please.

By now, ANNA *is begging.*

DIANNA: All right.

Anything to get her out of the house.

ANNA: A little script.
DIANNA: Alright, I'll get you something.

DIANNA *goes into her bathroom and returns with a bottle of pills.*

ANNA: What's this?
DIANNA: Here's a couple of Valiums. They're Valium fives. Now I want you to cut them in half before you take them.

ANNA *takes the pills.*

ANNA: I know Valium. I'll need both of them, believe me. (*The light dawns.*) That's your stash, isn't it?
DIANNA: Uh, ah.
ANNA: What else do you have in there?

She nods toward the bathroom and turns hard and cold.

DIANNA: I have my bathtub. I have my sink. I have my toothbrush.
ANNA: This is real interesting. You gave me this whole song-and-dance about how it's bad for me and you have your own stash. What are you on right now? Amphetamines?
DIANNA: I shoot up every day. Come on. It's time for you to go.

DIANNA'S *had it. She pushes* ANNA *toward the door.*

ANNA: I think you're a fucking hypocrite.
DIANNA: Let's go, Anna.
ANNA: No, I just do. You doctors, I feel like you're all alike. I appreciate this. But this is really amazing. How it's good for you and it's not for me. It's really interesting.
DIANNA: (*As cold as stone*) Try and get some rest, will you?

ANNA *knows she stepped over the line. She becomes contrite.*

ANNA: I'm sorry. I'm sorry, really I am.
DIANNA: It's okay. But you have to leave. I just have to get my work done. I've got to get it done. I'm really having a hard time.

Now it's DIANNA *who's begging.*

ANNA: Listen. I can't leave with you feeling like this.

DIANNA *plunks herself down in defeat. She cannot get rid of her friend.*

DIANNA: Oh, God.
ANNA: I can't. I wouldn't be able to get to sleep with a whole bottle of Valiums. Listen. Why don't you let me give you a massage? You're working so hard. You're always the one who's nurturing.

She starts rubbing DIANNA'S *neck.*

ANNA: Look how tense you are, you're like granite. You should take a Valium.
DIANNA: Give me yours.
ANNA: You've always been right there for me and I was so insensitive. I'm sorry. I really care about you.
DIANNA: That feels good.

ANNA *rubs* DIANNA'S *neck for a quiet, intimate moment. Then she leans in and kisses* DIANNA *on the neck.* DIANNA *goes stiff then pulls away.* ANNA *awkwardly stands there. Embarrassed. Rebuffed. Finally she says:*

ANNA: I guess I should go. I'm sorry. I'm really sorry. My mouth always—
DIANNA: —It's all right, Anna. I hope you can sleep.
ANNA: Thank you.
DIANNA: You're welcome. I'll call you tomorrow. Okay?

ANNA *doesn't really want to leave.*

ANNA: Should I close the door?
DIANNA: Yeah.
ANNA: I'll be home around six.
DIANNA: Okay.

ANNA *leaves.* DIANNA *is left alone.*

52. The Carpenter   DAY/INT.

The interview continues.

CARPENTER: I'm a girl, and as such I'm either treated as a nice girl who doesn't joke or banter with the guys, or I'm treated as someone who they can tell dirty jokes to. At first, they would curse and I would say, "Oh, forget it. I curse, too." But then I decided, no, I'm not going to say anything to them. You're either accepted as one of the guys and you get it all in one package, or you get none of it. There's no in-between. And I decided to be a nice girl 'cause I don't need any more hassles.

53. The Cable Splicer DAY/INT.

The interview continues.

CABLE SPLICER: There's all kinds of contradictions working with these guys in the garage. You know, I thought the better we got at our jobs, the more we'd be accepted. And respected. But in fact, it's had the opposite effect. This guy said to me not too long ago that he didn't really have pride in his job anymore because it was a job "a woman could do." On the other hand, these guys are really great to work with. There's all kinds of camaraderie in the garage. And you spend a lot of time with them. You really get to know them. I feel like they're really interested in me as a person. My life outside of the job. I'm remodeling the baby's room right now and they helped me do all the wiring and they're real interested in what I'm doing.

54. The Carpenter DAY/INT.

The interview continues.

CARPENTER: One day I had this conversation with this guy and he was talking about someone's big tits. And I said, "Women suffer a lot from the criticism they receive about their breasts." And the next day the pictures went up. And I don't mean pinups. The hard-core stuff. I went in. And in nailing up the pictures they'd nailed them through the crotches. They'd nailed them through the nipples and the crotches. So I walked in and said, "Who's the rapist here?" They ignored me. Finally I said, "Well, why don't you hang these up in the john, 'cause I don't want to come in and catch one of you jerking off or something." In a way, I didn't want them to know how I felt. 'Cause they'd just think, "If you can't stand the heat, get out of the kitchen." And I felt like screaming, "The kitchen needs to be redecorated for the new cooks."

55. The Doctor DAY/INT.

DIANNA'S *interview continues.*

DIANNA: Once when I was interning we had this girl who was brought in. She was seven years old, maybe younger. And she had been raped by her older brother's boyfriend, who was fifteen. And she didn't even know what had happened to her. She had excretions on her leg and a lot of pus coming from her vagina. And it turned out that not only had she been abused that one time, but she's complaining of this pain in her hand, an arthritis, which was due to a gynoccole infection. Which is clap. And that means this has been going on for months. And she didn't even have words for it. She called it, "we played love." Everybody knew what was going on. And the male pediatricians who were on duty at the time related to the whole thing by discussing how they'd done pelvic exams on very young girls, eight, nine, ten years old. And how when they tried to put the speculum in they would say to her, "Relax," and the kid would say back, "You mean, like I'm playing love?" Which of course meant that she had sex all the time. And they were obviously embarrassed and they were laughing and really trying to compete with each other to see who could tell the most sordid story. I was so angry. I started in on them and I said 20 percent of all sexually abused children were under six. And that 90 percent were girls who had been abused by adult males or teenage boys. And statistically it happened with just as much frequency in professional families as it did in the slums. We just didn't see them in city hospitals. I can't remember all that I said. But they reported me to the director, who called me into his office and really gave it to me. But in a very nice way. He told me that I had acted very immaturely. And that I had to learn how to handle my emotions if I was going to be a doctor. He said to me, "You're a doctor. Act like one."

56. Dianna's House. Bathroom. DAY/INT.

DIANNA *does the feminine thing and shaves her legs.* *who's judging?*

57. Gym.   DAY/INT.

DIANNA *moves from station to station lifting weights. By the end of the workout . . . she's exhausted.*

58. Restaurant   DAY/INT.

DIANNA *sits in a booth of the greasy spoon, reading the newspaper and sipping coffee.* ANNA *passes by the window and comes in. She pulls off her jacket and sits down.*

DIANNA: Hi. How are you?
ANNA: Not bad.

DIANNA: Great. I've been waiting for you. I have to tell you about this party I went to last night. It was wonderful. It was in the Hancock Building. You know where that is?
ANNA: Yeah. I think I know where it is.

ANNA'S *trying to listen but she's just not interested.*

DIANNA: Have you ever been there? Anyway, it was—

Her monologue's interrupted by the waitress carrying a pot of coffee.

LIL: How you doin'?
ANNA: Just pour it in. Pour it in, Lil.
DIANNA: Can I have some more tea water when you get a chance?
LIL: Sure. Know what you want?
ANNA: I'll have the usual.

LIL *leaves.*

DIANNA: Anyway. This was one of the best parties I've ever been to. For food, they had cheese sculptured like mermaids. Fabulous champagne. I wish you'd been there. It was wonderful.
ANNA: I don't wish I'd been there.

DIANNA *finally notices that something is wrong.*

DIANNA: What's with you, Anna? What's going on?

ANNA: I had a hard day.

DIANNA: Yeah?

ANNA: No, this one really takes the gold star.

DIANNA: What happened?

ANNA: Found out I didn't get the promotion.

DIANNA: What do you mean you didn't get the promotion?

ANNA: I didn't get the promotion.

DIANNA: What happened? What'd they tell you?

ANNA: They didn't tell me anything. It was all my fantasy. They hired a woman off the street. A woman with a college degree in business.

DIANNA: Oh, Anna.

ANNA: She's never even seen a truck in her life, I'm sure.

DIANNA: Oh, I'm sorry.

LIL *comes with their food.*

LIL: Here you go. Special.

ANNA: Thanks . . . I mean, the way I figure it is that they needed a woman, they didn't want me and so they hired her. And I can barely go back in there tomorrow.

DIANNA: And they didn't say one thing to you?

ANNA: No, no one said anything. You don't understand. It was my idea. The whole thing was my idea. And in the meantime, my head is turning to mush. See, I counted on this so much.

DIANNA: I know.

ANNA: Dianna, how is she gonna know, tell me, how's she gonna know how to interface ten drivers over a hundred and twenty-five miles in eight hours?

DIANNA: She's not. She's not going to know that.

ANNA: And once again, I have a boss who doesn't know his shit. Six years I stayed in the basement of that place. And I'm a nothing. Oh fuck, I can't even eat . . . The whole thing is, I know I can go in there. I can go in there tomorrow. The guys are used to me. They know me. I can walk in there to-morrow. I'd hire a swing shift tomorrow. I could walk right in and do it.

DIANNA: You know, the point is they don't want you to do it . . . do it well. They remember what they did to you when you started working there. They remember all the hard times they gave you and everything that they did to you. What if you did that back to them?

ANNA: I'd never do that.

DIANNA: I know you'd never do that but they don't know that. All they can see is what if we got her in there and she started doing it to us? They can't let that happen. They can't afford to have you do it. You changed everything for them, remember? Everything. All that you went through. You changed everything at that place. Nothing has ever been the same.

ANNA: And now I'm stuck. I'm stuck.

DIANNA: I know.

ANNA: Do you know how long I've counted on this thing?

DIANNA: I know. But you know what? You're never going to get that job. They'd never give it to you.

ANNA *starts to cry.*

ANNA: I want it.

DIANNA: I know, I know . . . Oh . . .

DIANNA *goes and slides into the booth beside* ANNA. *She comforts her friend, holding her in her arms.*

ANNA: Fucking shit.

DIANNA: Let's get out of here. Okay? Come on.

ANNA: Goddamn shit, I'm gonna quit.

ANNA *and* DIANNA *leave. As they pass in front of the window, they pause for a moment and embrace.*

59. Montage

 *Women working: A cable splicer rises through the air in her bucket; a worker on the line lifts a heavy steel chain and cuts it into small lengths; a scientist in her lab inspects the results of her latest experiment; a firefighter with brute strength opens a hydrant; a printer inks her press; a mail carrier delivers the mail.*

Credits Roll

This film contains fictitious characters with documentary footage of women at work. I would like to thank the women who were interviewed and filmed.

Virginia Alverez	IRONWORKER
Carol Becker	UNIVERSITY PROFESSOR
Ruth Belzer	UNIVERSITY ADMINISTRATOR
Chris Charlesworth	GRADUATE STUDENT, PHYSIOLOGY
Elaine Citron	EMERGENCY MEDICAL TECHNICIAN

Rose Davis	CHAIN INSPECTOR
Lisa DiCaprio	APPRENTICE CARPENTER
Mable Digby	MAIL CARRIER
JoAnn Elam	MAIL CARRIER
Susan Greene	CABLE SPLICING TECHNICIAN
Judy Hoffman	CAMERA ASSISTANT
Lauren Howard	FIREFIGHTER
Debra Howenstine	LANDSCAPER
Halli Lehrer	PRINTER
Julia Lesage	EDITOR
Judith Mayne	UNIVERSITY PROFESSOR
Susan Michmerhuizen	TRUCK DRIVER
Kathryn Mitchell	AIRLINE FIRST OFFICER
Patricia B. Murphy	SCULPTOR
Coral Norris	CARPENTER
Linda D. Pendleton	AIRLINE CAPTAIN
Margaret Roberts	CABLE SPLICING TECHNICIAN
Neena B. Schwartz	PHYSIOLOGIST
Barbara Stevko	PHYSICIAN
Elaine Stocker	NAPRAPATH
Lauren Sugarman	APPRENTICE ELEVATOR MECHANIC
Diane Suter	PHYSIOLOGIST
Ann van der Vort	PRODUCTION ASSISTANT
Babs H. Waldman	PHYSICIAN
Carole Warshaw	PHYSICIAN
Lola Wing	WOODSTRIPPER
Janet Zilai	BIOCHEMIST

and the men they work with . . .
Christopher Burke
David Feldman
Emanuel Fitzpatrick
Joe Hendrix
Jaime Gardiner
Ron Kirshenbaum
Gunnar Piotter
Paul Sardelle

CAST
Belinda Cloud	DOCTOR / Dianna
Donna Blue Lachman	TRUCK DRIVER / Anna

Helen Larimore	SCULPTOR
Mossetta Harris	CARPENTER
Fran Harth	PHILOSOPHY PROFESSOR
Jan Lucas	CABLE SPLICER
Lilly Ollinger	WAITRESS
Virginia Smiley	WOMAN IN STREET

PRODUCED, WRITTEN, EDITED, AND DIRECTED BY
Michelle Citron

CINEMATOGRAPHY
Frances Reid

ADDITIONAL CINEMATOGRAPHY
Michelle Citron
Greg Faller
Gordon Quinn
Ryszard Nykiel

LIGHTING
Matia Karrell

ADDITIONAL LIGHTING
Judy Hoffman

SOUND
Phoebe Bindiger

ADDITIONAL SOUND
Anne Leighton
Ellen Seiter

CAMERA ASSISTANT
Judy Hoffman

ADDITIONAL CAMERA ASSISTANT
Michael Niederman

ORIGINAL MUSIC COMPOSED AND ARRANGED BY
Karin Pritikin

ADDITIONAL MUSIC
Donna Blue Lachman

EDITOR
Michelle Citron

ASSISTANT EDITOR
Carol Medina

PRODUCTION MANAGER
Eileen Fitzpatrick

PRODUCTION ASSISTANTS

Jae Alexander	Anne Leighton
Doreen Bartoni	Lilly Ollinger
Deborah Bloom	Liz Schillinger
Cathy Christoff	Virginia Smiley
Candice Bullard	Claudia Springer
Abby Darrow-Sherman	Chris Straayer
Greg Faller	Tulin Yilbar

MUSICIANS

Bill Gilardon	Trombones
Audrey Morrison	English Horn, Oboe
Jean Oelrich	English Horn, Oboe
T.C. Furlong	Pedal Steel Guitar
George Sawyer	Guitar
Steve Shields	Bass
Bill Byran	Drums
Karin Pritikin	Piano
Bill Gilardon	Additional Orchestration
Steve Rashid	Engineer
Q & R Studios	Recording

Nancy Zucker / Mixed Media	Titles
Ric Coken / Zenith / dB	Sound Mixer
Kinetics / Optifex	Opticals
Allied Film Lab / Chicago	Film Lab
Lucille Peak	Negative Cutter
Executive Catering / Chicago	Caterer
Kathy Weber	Still Photographer
and	
Patricia B. Murphy	Sculpture

MUSIC
"I'm Crazy (for Chasin' after You)"
Music and lyrics by Karin Pritikin. Copyright 1983
Sung by Paula Lazarus

"I Just Can't Go Home Again"
Music and lyrics by Karin Pritikin. Copyright 1983
Sung by Karin Pritikin

"Haiti"
Composed and performed by Donna Blue Lachman. Copyright 1983

This film was funded in part by grants from the National Endowment
for the Arts and Northwestern University, School of Speech, Alumni
Fund.

Acknowledgments

A book is never, truly, the work of a sole author. My debt and gratitude to:

Joanie Albrecht, Annette Barbier, Fina Bathrick, Leo Charney, Dwight Conquergood, Patricia Erens, Tom Gunning, Laura Kipnis, Chuck Kleinhans, Matia Karrell, Rachel Lyon, Judith Mayne, Rick Maxwell, Michael Renov, Jonathan Shay, Elizabeth Wilson, and Debbie Zimmerman for insightful feedback, useful tidbits, good friendship, and much-needed moral support during various stages of my long book-writing process; and Robert Bumsted, Richard Davison, Marc Dunn, and Lewis Smith for their wisdom about the body;

Valerie Fashman and Paula Sjogerman for their brilliance in performing the parts of Dora I and Dora II in "Speaking the Unspeakable" in its earlier incarnation as a performance piece; and Adrienne Kaplan for her sensitive portrayal of the "Grandmother" in "The Simple Act of Seeing" when it, too, was a performance piece;

Ted and Luann Van Zelst for their generosity in endowing the Van Zelst Research Professor of Communications Chair, School of Speech, Northwestern University, which gave me fifteen months precious time away from teaching to begin this book; the Center for Interdisciplinary Research in the Arts, Northwestern University and the School of Speech Alumni Fund, Northwestern University, David H. Zarefsky, Dean, for providing the financial resources necessary to bring images into this text;

Stu Baker and Claire Dougherty, Media Development Lab, Northwestern University, for opening the door to visualizing this text; and Jim Ferolo, artist and digitizer extraordinaire, for helping to create the images;

Jonathan Matson and Micah Kleit for believing in this book; Linda Lincoln for her sensitive pen; Amy Unger for her sophisticated eye.

Most of all, this book couldn't have been written without:

Carole Warshaw, who provided friendship and intellectual comradeship; Anne Avery, who taught me how to see;

Edith Citron and Samuel Citron, my parents, who always showed unending love and faith in their children; my sister Vicki Citron, confidant, best friend, and intellectual companion;

and Susan Michmerhuizen, who for twenty years has shown me the way, filled my heart, sharpened my words, and kept me honest.

Notes

What's Wrong with This Picture?

1. Laurie Ouellette, "Camcorders R Us," *The Independent* (May 1994): 34–38.
2. John Kuiper, "A Note on Research in Progress: A Search for the Sources for Amateur Motion Pictures," *The Journal of Film and Video* 38, no. 3–4 (summer–fall 1986): 37–38.
3. Patricia R. Zimmermann, *Reel Families: A Social History of Amateur Film* (Bloomington: Indiana University Press, 1995) provides an extensive story of corporate America's relationship to amateur picture making from the mid-nineteenth century to the present. Part of her argument is that the history of amateur filmmaking negotiates the boundaries between amateurism and professionalism, and between corporate capitalism and the private place of the home.
4. Popular culture also plays a role in teaching us what to shoot. See Chuck Kleinhans's study of the influence of the *Keystone Kops, Jaws, Star Wars,* and *The Sound of Music* on his aunt's home movies. Chuck Kleinhans, "Aunt Alice's Home Movies," *Journal of Film and Video* 38, no. 3–4 (summer–fall 1986): 25–35. Zimmermann makes a compelling argument for the economic and aesthetic interdependence of Hollywood and home-movie filmmaking. Hollywood film techniques and production processes were actively promoted for the amateur filmmaker through articles in mass market and film magazines, as well as in marketing promotions.
5. Judith Williamson, *Consuming Passions: The Dynamics of Popular Culture* (London: Marion Boyars, 1986), 123. In a twist, Patricia Zimmermann describes two Hollywood films—*Down and Out in Beverly Hills* (1986) and *Cousins* (1989)—in which the male child turns the family's home video camera back on his parents, revealing the secrets most home videos conceal. Both Williamson and Zimmermann further argue that home-movie practices, and their resulting image memories, serve an ideological function beyond the parent/child power dynamic. Home images obscure class as well as other kinds of social differences and promote the nuclear family as the place of leisure and the center of all meaningful activity. In these ways, home images encourage a retreat from social and political participation.
6. Clearly I am talking about photographic images that haven't been altered after the moment of picture taking itself.
7. Mark McKinnon, "High-Concept Media," *Campaigns and Elections* 13, no. 5 (January 1993): 49.
8. Patricia Erens, "Home Movies in Commercial Narrative Film," *Journal of Film and Video* 38, no. 3–4 (summer–fall 1986): 99.
9. Patricia R. Zimmermann, "The Amateur, the Avant-Garde, and Ideologies of Art," *Journal of Film and Video* 38, no. 3–4 (summer–fall 1986): 81.
10. Therapists who practice a kind of photo-therapy find that "during periods of stress and family crisis . . . there is a sharp drop in the number of pictures taken. This includes periods surrounding illness, death, family separations and fragmentations, and heightened conflict between different members and fractions of the family. . . . Periods of depression, crisis, disorganization, and rapid family change are often characterized by the absence of pictures. Gaps in the picture chronology can point to questions to be asked about loss, separation, disappointment, and grief." Florence W. Kaslow and Jack Friedman, "Utilization of Family Photos and Movies in Family Therapy," *Journal of Marriage and Family Counseling* (January 1977): 20, 23.
11. There are clear patterns to the imagery we shoot. Anthropologist Richard Chalfen studied two hundred collections of home-movie imagery: photographs, home movies, and home videos made

mostly by white, middle-class families in the northeastern part of the United States between 1940 and 1980. He found he could sort all private "home" images into four categories: vacation activity (including traveling, picnics, going to the beach, playing on swings); holiday activity (Christmas, Thanksgiving, Halloween); special events (birthday parties, bar mitzvahs, communions, a parade or sports event with a family member); and local activity (unusual events such as showing off something new, baby's first steps, driving the new car). Richard Chalfen, *Snapshot Versions of Life* (Bowling Green, Ohio: Bowling Green State University Popular Press, 1987).

12. Zimmermann describes the political use of home-video technology by gay and lesbian videomakers. Zimmermann, *Reel Families*, pp. 154–6.

Speaking the Unspeakable

1. Paul Fussell, *The Great War and Modern Memory* (London: Oxford University Press, 1975), 169. For an in-depth and eloquent discussion of war trauma and its aftermath, see Jonathan Shay, *Achilles in Vietnam: Combat Trauma and the Undoing of Character* (New York: Atheneum, 1994).

2. Ellen Bass and Laura Davis, *The Courage to Heal: A Guide for Women Survivors of Child Sexual Abuse* (New York: Harper and Row, 1988), 66.

3. Ibid., 84.

4. L. Meyer Williams, "Adult Memories of Child Sexual Abuse: Placing Sexual Assault in Long-Term Perspective," *Trauma and Tragedy: The Origins, Management and Prevention of Traumatic Stress in Today's World*, World Conference of the International Society for Traumatic Stress Studies, Amsterdam, 1992. See also Williams, "Recall of Childhood Trauma: A Prospective Study of Women's Memories of Child Sexual Abuse," *Journal of Consulting and Clinical Psychology* 62 (1994): 1167–76; and Williams, "Recovered Memories of Abuse in Women with Documented Child Sexual Victimization Histories," *Journal of Traumatic Stress* 8 (1995): 649–74.

5. Jacqueline Rose, *Sexuality in the Field of Vision* (London: Verso, 1986), 12–15. See also, Janet Walker," 'I Don't Remember Anything Like That': Trauma, Transference and Memory in Psychological Films" (paper presented at the Psychoanalysis and Cinema Conference, UCLA, 1993). Walker has a good analysis of how children are assaulted and also desire.

6. Judith Herman, *Trauma and Recovery: The Aftermath of Violence—From Domestic Abuse to Political Terror* (New York: Basic Books, 1991): 7–32. Herman argues, correctly I think, that all moments of public discussion of trauma—hysteria, war, incest, political terrorism—are historically specific and tied to particular political movements.

7. Diana Russell, *The Secret Trauma: Incest in the Lives of Girls and Women* (New York: Basic Books, 1986). I have deliberately chosen a study that predates the current debates about incest.

8. Cited in Mic Hunter, *Abused Boys: The Neglected Victims of Sexual Abuse* (Lexington, Mass.: Lexington Books, 1990), 26; A. Bell and M. Wienberg, (Bloomington, Ind.: Institute for Sex Research, N. D.) Mimeo cited in Hunter, *Abused Boys*; D. Finkelhor, *Sexually Victimized Children* (New York: Free Press, 1979); G. Fritz, K. Stoll, and N. Wagner, "A Comparison of Males and Females Who Were Sexually Molested as Children," *Journal of Sex and Marital Therapy* 7 (1981): 54–59; G. Kercher and M. McShane, "The Prevalence of Child Sexual Abuse, Victimization in an Adult Sample of Texas Residents," Sam Houston State University, Huntsville, 1983, cited in Hunter, *Abused Boys*. The range of frequency is due to inconsistent reporting caused by cultural factors such as myths about masculinity, including the reluctance to see males as victims. For books on male sexual abuse, see Hunter as well as Mike Lew, *Victims No Longer: Men Recovering from Incest and Other Sexual Child Abuse* (New York: Harper and Row, 1990).

9. This type of memory was best described by Frederic C. Bartlett, *Remembering: A Study in Experimental and Social Psychology* (London: Cambridge University Press, 1932). See also Ulric Neisser, "John Dean's Memory: A Case Study," *Cognition* 9, no. 1 (1981): 1–22. For a detailed explication of the different types of memory, see Jennifer H. Freyd, *Betrayal Trauma: The Logic of Forgetting Childhood Abuse* (Cambridge: Harvard University Press, 1996), 79–127. Freyd presents the current research on memory in all of its complexities, including a well-argued, empirically based response to the issue of inaccurate and "false" memory.

10. Bass, *Courage to Heal*, 72.

11. The work of Bessel van der Kolk is centrally concerned with the role of neurohormones in trauma. See "The Body Keeps the Score: Approaches to the Psychobiology of Post-traumatic Stress Disorder" and "Trauma and Memory," in *Traumatic Stress: The Effects of Overwhelming Experience on Mind, Body, and Society*, eds. Bessel A. van der Kolk, Alexander C. McFarlane, and Lars Weisaeth (New York: The Guilford Press, 1996). For a comprehensive discussion of the interrelationship between physiology, psychology, biology, and the social world, see Bessel van der Kolk, *Psychological Trauma* (Washington D.C.: American Psychiatric Press, 1987).

12. Freyd, *Betrayal Trauma*, 79–127. I am emphasizing trauma that is both terrifying and fearful. But as Freyd so clearly lays out, memory is a complex and multifaceted process. There are many

ways of both forgetting and remembering; furthermore, not all forgotten and remembered experiences are fear induced.

13. Sylvia Fraser, *My Father's House* (New York: Ticknor and Fields, 1988), 220.
14. The cognitive model can be found in M. Horowitz, *Stress Response Syndromes* (Northvale, N.J.: Jason Aronson, 1986), 93–94. The emotional model can be found in P. Russell, "Trauma, Repetition and Affect" (paper presented at Psychiatry Grand Rounds, Cambridge Hospital, Cambridge, Mass., September 5, 1990).
15. I thank Carole Warshaw for this insight.
16. Louise Kaplan, *Female Perversions: The Temptations of Emma Bovary* (New York: Doubleday, 1991). Kaplan goes to great lengths to distinguish a sexual perversion, i.e., a behavior that elevates an anxiety, from the same behavior that is a voluntary desire between consenting adults. She cautions that behavior itself can't be easily categorized, stressing that only in context can you hope to know its meanings.
17. See Fraser, as well as *She Who Was Lost Is Remembered: Healing from Incest through Creativity*, ed. Louis M. Wisechild (Seattle: Seal Press, 1991). In that book, see especially Catherine Houser, "Writing as an Act of Healing," and Judy Grahn, "March to the Mother Sea: Healing Poems of Baby Girls Raped at Home." I count my own film work, especially *Daughter Rite* and *What You Take For Granted* . . . in this category.
18. The video therapy described here was developed by Louis W. Trinnin, Trauma Recovery Institute, Morgantown, W.Va. It was conducted with a group of patients who presented with post-traumatic stress disorder or dissociative disorders. All the patients had confirmed traumas, either combat trauma, childhood abuse, and/or incest. L. Bills and Louis W. Trinnin, "Resolving the Fixed Idea 100 Years Later" (paper presented at "Trauma and Tragedy: The Origins, Management and Prevention of Traumatic Stress in Today's World," The World Conference of the International Society for Traumatic Stress Studies, Amsterdam, 1992). Further information about this therapy can be obtained at http://access.mountain.net/~trauma. Web site address current as of April 1998.
19. An interesting issue to explore would be the role of video specifically in this process. For instance, is there something about our experiences and expectations of television narrative itself that is an essential part of the process?
20. Pierre Janet, *Psychological Healing*, trans. E. Paul and C. Paul (New York: Macmillan, 1925): 661–3.
21. For an extended analysis of the relationship between aesthetic choices and audience response to my early experimental work, see my article "Women's Film Production: Going Mainstream" in *Female Spectators: Looking at Film and Television*, ed. E. Deidre Pribram (London: Verso Press, 1988).

The Simple Act of Seeing

1. Eva Hoffman, *Lost in Translation* (New York: Penguin Books, 1989), 211–12.

The Story in 1969 . . .

1. Emily Dickinson, "Hope Is the Thing with Feathers," *The Complete Poems of Emily Dickinson*, ed. Thomas H. Johnson (Boston: Little, Brown and Company, 1960).

The Story in 1956 . . .

1. The version of "The Three Sillies" read to me by my father came from *Through Fairy Halls*, vol. 6 of *My Book House*, ed. Olive Beaupre Miller (Chicago: The Book House for Children, 1950).

The Story in 1997 . . .

1. Ian Hacking, *Rewriting the Soul: Multiple Personality and the Sciences of Memory* (Princeton: Princeton University Press, 1995).

Selected Bibliography

Barthes, Roland. *Camera Lucida: Reflections on Photography*. Trans. Richard Howard. New York: Farrar, Straus and Giroux, 1981.

Berger, John. *About Looking*. New York: Vintage Books, 1980.

———. *Another Way of Telling*. New York: Pantheon Books, 1982.

Breuer, Joseph, and Sigmund Freud. *Studies on Hysteria*. Vol. 2 of *The Standard Edition of the Complete Psychological Works of Sigmund Freud*, ed. and trans. James Strachey. London: Hogarth Press, 1955.

Chalfen, Richard. *Snapshot Versions of Life*. Bowling Green, Ohio: Bowling Green State University Popular Press, 1987.

Fraser, Sylvia. *My Father's House*. New York: Ticknor and Fields, 1988.

Freud, Sigmund. "Aetiology of Hysteria." Vol. 3 of *The Standard Edition of the Complete Psychological Works of Sigmund Freud*, ed. and trans. James Strachey. London: Hogarth Press, 1962.

———. *Dora: An Analysis of a Case of Hysteria*. New York: Macmillan, 1963.

Freud, Sophie. *My Three Mothers and Other Passions*. New York: New York University Press, 1988.

Freyd, Jennifer H. *Betrayal Trauma: The Logic of Forgetting Childhood Abuse*. Cambridge: Harvard University Press, 1996.

Fussell, Paul. *The Great War and Modern Memory*. London: Oxford University Press, 1975.

Hacking, Ian. *Rewriting the Soul: Multiple Personality and the Sciences of Memory*. Princeton: Princeton University Press, 1995.

Herman, Judith. *Father-Daughter Incest*. Cambridge: Harvard University Press, 1982.

———. *Trauma and Recovery. The Aftermath of Violence—From Domestic Abuse to Political Terror*. New York: Basic Books, 1991.

Janet, Pierre. *Psychological Healing*. Trans. E. Paul and C. Paul. New York: Macmillan, 1925.

Journal of Film and Video 38, no. 3–4 (summer–fall 1986).

Kaplan, Louise. *Female Perversions: The Temptations of Emma Bovary*. New York: Doubleday, 1991.

Lesy, Michael. "snapshots: psychological documents, frozen dreams." *Afterimage* 4, no. 4 (October 1976): 12–13.

Lorde, Audre. *A Burst of Light*. Ithaca: Firebrand Books, 1988.

Masson, Jeffrey M. *The Assault on Truth: Freud's Suppression of the Seduction Theory*. New York: Farrar, Straus and Giroux, 1984.

Nussbaum, Martha C. *The Fragility of Goodness: Luck and Ethics in Greek Tragedy and Philosophy*. London: Cambridge University Press, 1986.

O'Brien, Tim. *The Things They Carried*. New York: Penguin Books, 1990.

Olsen, Tillie. *Silences*. New York: Dell Publishing, 1978.

Rich, Adrienne. *Of Woman Born: Motherhood as Experience and Institution*. New York: Bantam Books, 1977.

———. *On Lies, Secrets, and Silence*. New York: Norton, 1979.

Rose, Jacqueline. *Sexuality in the Field of Vision*. London: Verso, 1986.

Rush, Florence. "The Freudian Cover-up." *Chrysalis* 1 (1977): 31–45.

Russell, Diana. *The Secret Trauma: Incest in the Lives of Girls and Women*. New York: Basic Books, 1986.

Sarton, May. *Mrs. Stevens Hears the Mermaids Singing*. New York: Norton, 1975.

Schafer, Roy. *Retelling a Life: Narration and Dialogue in Psychoanalysis*. New York: Basic Books, 1992.

Shay, Jonathan. *Achilles in Vietnam: Combat Trauma and the Undoing of Character*. New York: Atheneum, 1994.

Sontag, Susan. *On Photography*. New York: Farrar, Straus and Giroux, 1977.

Steedman, Carolyn. *Past Tenses: Essays on Writing, Autobiography, and History*. London: Rivers Oram Press, 1992.

Styron, William. *Darkness Visible*. New York: Vintage Books, 1990.

Terr, Lenore. *Unchained Memories. True Stories of Traumatic Memories, Lost and Found*. New York: Basic Books, 1994.

Vidal, Gore. *Palimpsest*. New York: Penguin Books, 1995.

Williamson, Judith. *Consuming Passions: The Dynamics of Popular Culture*. London: Marion Boyars, 1986.

Zeitlin, Steven J., Amy J. Kotkin, and Holly Cutting-Baker. *A Celebration of American Family Folklore*. Washington, D.C.: Smithsonian Institute, 1982.

Zimmermann, Patricia R. *Reel Families: A Social History of Amateur Film*. Bloomington: Indiana University Press, 1995.

MICHELLE CITRON is professor of Radio/Television/Film at Northwestern University, where she is also director of the Center for Interdisciplinary Research in the Arts and former chair of the Department of Radio/TV/ Film. She is an award-winning filmmaker whose work includes *Daughter Rite,* a ground-breaking narrative film. Her films, distributed in seven countries, have been screened at film festivals and museums worldwide and are in the permanent collections of over two hundred universities and film schools. She has received grants from the National Endowment for the Arts, the National Endowment for the Humanities, and two fellowships from the Illinois Arts Council.